# Railway Memori...

# DONCASTER

## *Derek Porter & Stephen Chapman*

**BELLCODE BOOKS**
10 RIDGE BANK
TODMORDEN
WEST YORKSHIRE OL14 7BA

Copyright © 1997 Bellcode Books
ISBN 1 871233 09 7

Edited by Stephen Chapman

Printed by The Amadeus Press Ltd., Huddersfield.

**ABOVE:** Sandringham Class B17/1 4-6-0 No. 61643 *Champion Lodge* makes a spectacular start from platform two at the south end of Doncaster Central station with the 9.7am stopping train to Peterborough via Lincoln on 31st August, 1954. (*Brian Morrison*)

**FRONTICEPIECE:** In the 1950s, Doncaster B1 4-6-0 No. 61145 awaits departure from the then platform five with an Up express formed of blood and custard liveried Gresley coaches. (*N.E.Stead collection*)

**FRONT COVER:** Happy days on the platform at Doncaster. Spotless A3 4-6-2 No. 60091 *Captain Cuttle* - still with its single chimney and round dome - coasts through Central station with another Up express formed 'blood and custard' Gresley coaches on a sunny day in 1952. (*The late W. Oliver/Colour-Rail*)

**BACK COVER TOP:** The days of blood and custard coaches were numbered by the time this view was recorded. Black-liveried V2 2-6-2 No. 60914 passes the Plant works while setting off with a southbound express in 1958. (*Geoff Warnes/Colour-Rail*)

**BACK COVER BOTTOM:** One of Doncaster's most distinguished products, LNER A4 4-6-2 No. 4468 *Mallard*, holder of the world speed record for steam, receives admirers while stood outside the Plant Works paint shop during an open day on 17th June, 1978. (*Stephen Chapman*)

# INTRODUCTION

Mention Doncaster to anyone and unless they follow the sport of kings they will likely as not think of railways.

Producing the world's fastest and most famous steam locomotives put Doncaster at the front of people's minds but while the locomotive works - the Plant as it is known locally - was a major part of the railway scene, there was much more to this South Yorkshire railway metropolis.

It was - and still is - an important crossroads on the East Coast Main Line, its approach from the south flanked by extensive marshalling yards, workshops and locomotive sheds. It is still the point where express and Pullman trains leave the main line for Hull and the West Riding.

There was even more which passengers never saw. Beyond the rows of houses, the factories and marshlands, out among the pit heaps was a network of freight lines built to move endless tonnages of coal from the many collieries sunk in the early 20th century to make Doncaster as much a centre of mining as railways and racing.

In **Railway Memories No. 10** 170 photographs by former Plant and Carr wagon works railwayman Derek Porter and other

distinguished photographers recall the times when grimy goods engines and fussy little Great Northern tank engines on pilot work mingled with polished Pacifics heading the most famous expresses.

Coverage has been extended along the Leeds line as far as Fitzwilliam to meet up with Railway Memories No.6.

## Contents

This engine was not built at Doncaster, was rarely seen there and is pictured here at March shed on 27th March, 1959. But B17/4 4-6-0 No. 61657 carried the name of the town's illustrious football team across East Anglia. *Doncaster Rovers*, built at Darlington in 1936, was scrapped at Stratford works, London, in June, 1960. (*Neville Stead*)

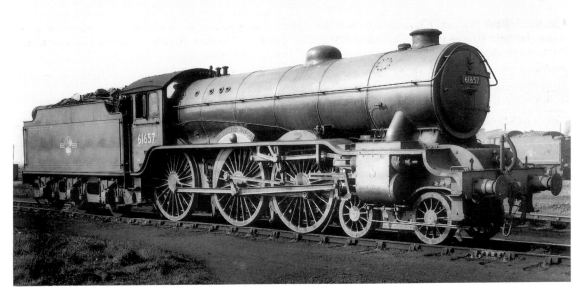

# SETTING THE SCENE

For more than 140 years Doncaster has been a railway centre of renown, but it came close to being little more than a fairly minor junction on a cross-country line.

In its efforts to build a main line from London to York the Great Northern Railway encountered tough opposition in Parliament from George Hudson, the so-called Railway King, who was determined to protect the monopoly of his established route from Euston.

Furthermore, one early Great Northern scheme aimed to by-pass Doncaster by continuing the original Peterborough, Boston and Lincoln route direct from Gainsborough to Selby and York.

But for the determination of the GNR backers and especially the West Riding MP Edmund Denison, who later became the company's chairman, the East Coast Main Line as it is now might not have been built and Doncaster might not have taken its place in railway history.

Despite all the obstacles put in its way during a two-year Parliamentary battle, the Great Northern's London and York Bill for 327 miles of new railway finally received the Royal Assent in June, 1846.

It was, however, another six years before the present main line reached Doncaster, the Boston and Lincoln loop being the first built. It reached Gainsborough in April, 1849 wher it connected with the Manchester, Sheffield and Lincolnshire Railway.

During this time the Great Northern set up a locomotive repair works at Boston - it did not build its own locomotives then.

Main line railways first reached Doncaster around 1850, 11 years after York and 15 years after Leeds, when the South Yorkshire Railway came in from Barnsley and the GNR opened its line from Retford to Askern, 6.5 miles north of Doncaster. The two met at Doncaster South Junction but had separate stations, the GN's being where the present one is while South Yorkshire trains initially used Cherry Tree Lane, later known as St. James Bridge.

At Askern, the GN joined the Lancashire and Yorkshire Railway's new branch from Knottingley but to continue beyond there to York it was forced to seek running powers over Hudson's York and North Midland Railway.

Nevertheless, some semblance of a King's Cross - York route was in place, even if it did involve a grand tour via Boston, Lincoln, Retford, Doncaster and Knottingley.

By 1852, though, completion of the GNR line between Peterborough, Grantham and Retford finally created the present direct route from London to Doncaster.

Then, after nearly choosing Peterborough, the GNR moved its locomotive works to Doncaster in 1853 and the Plant was founded.

The South Yorkshire Railway continued to push eastwards and by 1859 it had opened a line from Marshgate to Keadby, North Lincolnshire, completing the route to Scunthorpe and Grimsby although the section to Thorne was realigned under further powers acquired by the SY between 1862 and 1866. It was quadrupled in 1912.

By the 1860s, Doncaster was becoming established as a major railway crossroads but there was plenty more to come, even though the Railway Mania which spawned so many new lines was over.

In 1866 the West Riding and Grimsby Railway(owned jointly by the Great Northern and the Manchester, Sheffield and Lincolnshire Railway which absorbed the South Yorkshire in 1874) was opened. Running from Stainforth and Hatfield(on the Grimsby line) and Marshgate to Wakefield, it gave the GN direct access to West Yorkshire where it established its own extensive network. The legs from Marshgate and Stainforth met at Adwick Junction, Carcroft, and the WR&G allowed through running not only between those places in its name but also between King's Cross, Wakefield, Leeds and Bradford without using other companies' lines.

Another significant railway was in place the following year when the GN connected Gainsborough to the direct Retford line at Black Carr Junction, completing the GN and Great Eastern Joint line from East Anglia.

But 1867 was an auspicious year for another reason - the Plant built its first locomotive. The Class F2 0-4-2 No. 18 designed by Patrick Stirling was the first in a distinguished line of 2,223 locomotives ending with the last BR Class 58 freight diesel in April, 1987.

At its peak, the Plant covered 84 acres and employed 4,000 people building and repairing locomotives, coaches and wagons. Most of this activity was hidden from the station by the long block of works offices where many a famous locomotive and coach design was created.

The next railway on the scene was the North Eastern Railway's Hull and Doncaster line which opened in 1869 and connected the Hull

Near the site of Doncaster's first station, ex-Great Central J11 0-6-0 No. 64302 of Mexborough shed passes St. James Bridge station while heading a westbound excursion in the early 1950s. The train is about to pass over St. James Junction with Cherry Tree Lane goods depot in the left background. *(G. Oats)*

-Selby line to the Doncaster-Grimsby at Thorne. As its name spells out, this line afforded direct access between Hull, Goole and Doncaster.

The NER was formed in 1854 when the GN's bitter rival, the York and North Midland merged with other companies. Unlike the YNM, the NER became the GN's most loyal partner and together they developed the East Coast main line into the premier high speed route it is today.

A key move by the NER was the opening in 1871 of its direct line from York via Selby to the GN's Askern line at Shaftholme Junction, immediately north of the intersection with the West Riding and Grimsby.

Out among the fields, Shaftholme Junction became something of a landmark, being the boundary between the GN and NE companies and, from 1948 to 1967, between the Eastern and North Eastern regions of British Railways.

In 1877, a spur was installed from the York line at Joan Croft Junction to the WR&G at Applehurst Junction enabling direct running between York and South Humberside. It was a short but vital link for freight traffic and remained so in 1997.

With the principal lines in place, the first phase in Doncaster's railway development was complete. More railways followed in the early 20th Century when new deep coal mines were sunk to tap the rich Barnsley seam 2,000ft or more below ground.

In 1908 the Great Central Railway(which the Manchester, Sheffield and Lincolnshire became in 1899 following the opening of its main line to London) opened a 1.5-mile single track to Brodsworth Colliery from a north-facing junction on the WR&G at Castle Hills, between Bentley and Carcroft. In the early 1960s a south-facing curve was added so that coal trains could run directly between the colliery and Thorpe Marsh power station.

In 1910, under the same Act of Parliament, the GC opened a spur from Carcroft Junction to Skellow Junction, on the Adwick-Stainforth line, so that coal could be brought south from the new Bullcroft Colliery.

Also opened by the GC in 1910 was the Doncaster avoiding line from Hexthorpe Junction, on the Mexborough line, to Bentley Junction, on the Grimsby line where a flying junction was built to ease the flow of traffic. It allowed the increasingly heavy goods traffic between South Yorkshire, Scunthorpe and Immingham to by-pass Doncaster station, a role it still fulfilled in 1997.

One of the more significant of the 'new' lines,

**Class A4 Pacific No. 60034 *Lord Farringdon* passes over Shaftholme Junction and crosses from the Eastern to the North Eastern Region of BR with a northbound East Coast express on 29th May, 1961. Going to the right is the Askern branch while a WD 2-8-0 heads an eastbound coal train along the West Riding and Grimsby line from Adwick to Stainforth.** *(Peter Rose)*

and one which retains some importance as the 20th Century draws to a close, is the South Yorkshire Joint Railway from Dinnington, near Worksop, to Kirk Sandall Junction on the Doncaster-Grimsby line. A joint venture by five companies - the GN, GC, NE, L&Y and Midland -it provided a direct link for export coal from Nottinghamshire to Immingham, Goole and Hull and was fully open by 1909/13. It crossed over the ECML at Black Carr with connections in the Doncaster direction from junctions at St. Catherine's and Low Ellers. It carried a sparse passenger service until 1929, after which the stations were used only by excursions. There were no passenger trains between St. Catherine's and Kirk Sandall but from 1924 the line served Markham Main Colliery.

Another new line reaching Doncaster at Black Carr was the Lancashire and Yorkshire's Dearne Valley route from Crofton, near Wakefield. Opened between 1908 and 1909 it joined the Lincoln line at Bessacarr Junction after crossing over the ECML on a large girder bridge. It served Yorkshire Main Colliery and had connections from the South Yorkshire Joint at St. Catherine's. From 1912 the DV ran a steam railmotor passenger service between Wakefield Kirkgate and Edlington Halt, Warmsworth. Corporation trams provided the only link with Doncaster itself. In the same locality, the GNR opened its branch from

Loversall to Rossington Colliery in 1913 and in 1996 both pit and railway were still open.

The other notable railway built during this period was the Hull & Barnsley and Great Central Joint running from the H&B main line at Aire Junction, Gowdall, through Sprotborough and Warmsworth to Braithwell Junction, between Rotherham and Worksop. Like the SYJ, its aim was to take coal from Nottinghamshire collieries to Hull for export.

The whole line opened in 1916, including a 1.75-mile branch from Bullcroft Junction, about three miles north west of Doncaster as the crow flies, to Bullcroft Colliery. This was not without some difficulties and delays, especially on the section south of Bullcroft Junction. Not only did it have to cut through the limestone ridge around Warmsworth, passing under the Doncaster - Mexborough line in a deep cutting, it had, like the avoiding line, to cross the River Don on a substantial lattice girder bridge. The joint and avoiding lines ran parallel at Sprotborough where connections were made between the two.

Generally everything north of Bullcroft Junction was worked by the H&B, and everything to the south by the GC. Bullcroft Junction itself became an 'out of town' railway centre complete with two-road timber loco shed, turntable, and sidings where engines were changed and coal trains brought together for staging and marshalling.

The scheme included its own terminus in Doncaster for passenger trains as well as goods traffic. To this end, a short branch was laid from a triangular junction with the H&B and GC Joint to York Road which was situated immediately below the embankment carrying the avoiding line. The triangle, located between Bullcroft and Sprotborough junctions, was named Doncaster Junction. An island platform was built but no roof. As well as general goods facilities, sidings served the Co-op dairy and bakery, and a petrol depot.

Alas, York Road remained goods only for its entire life but it did survive until late 1979 by which time its was occupied by a scrapyard.

Doncaster had two more general freight terminals besides York Road and the GNR depot next to Central station. The GC depot was at Marshgate and the old South Yorkshire Railway depot at Cherry Tree Lane appears to have been used by the Midland(as was the station) - 1920s Ordnance Survey maps showing it as London Midland and Scottish Railway, the Midland's successor after the 1923 grouping.

That particular event also saw the formation of the London and North Eastern Railway through merger of the GNR, GCR, NER(which took over the H&B in 1922), the Great Eastern and other railways in Scotland.

Other goods facilities in Doncaster included a branch from Marshgate serving factories on the Wheatley Park industrial estate, the biggest of which was the Ford tractor plant, now owned by Case - International Harvesters.

Under the 1960s BR Freight Sundries Plan which concentrated such traffic on a few main depots, Doncaster Central was to be the only depot besides Lincoln covering the whole of Lincolnshire and the Doncaster area, but unlike Lincoln, it had no modern handling equipment, relying on traditional labour-intensive methods. By the 1990s the railway's only freight terminal was at Belmont Sidings, Balby.

Some 20 private sidings in the immediate Doncaster area included those serving the Pilkington's and Rockware glassworks at Kirk Sandall, the town gas works and council depot, both at Marshgate, British Ropes and other factories at Belmont, and quarries at Warmsworth. Substantial local goods traffic through Doncaster came from Harworth Glass Bulbs on the South Yorkshire Joint which in the 1960s amounted to 40-50 wagonloads every weekday, including ferry vans for export via Harwich or Dover. There were also maltings at Barnby Dun, Bramwith and Carcroft.

The heavy goods and mineral traffic demanded five marshalling yards in Doncaster plus facilities for the repair and construction of wagons. Besides the railway company's own facility, there were three other private wagon works in Hexthorpe - the Danum Wagon Co., Thos. Burnett's, and Wagon Repairs Ltd.

By the 1880s the workload at the Plant was so heavy that major expansion was necessary. To release capacity for dealing with more locomotives and passenger rolling stock, and to reduce congestion in the station area with wagons going in and out of the Plant, the GNR decided to build a new wagon works two miles to the south at Carr, transferring all wagon building and repairs there in 1889. The Carr works stayed in business until 1965 when its operations were moved back to the Plant.

Over the years there were no fewer than five

As it passed along the east side of Doncaster, the South Yorkshire Joint line served Markham Main Colliery.
Steam, in the form of 0-6-0ST *Arthur*, Hunslet No. 3782 built in 1953, worked on there until the mid-1970s. *Arthur* is seen shunting on 3rd June, 1971.
*(Adrian Booth)*

**Above: The highlight of any day at Doncaster was the passage of a crack train like the Queen of Scots Pullman which ran from King's Cross to Glasgow Queen Street via Leeds and Harrogate. On 30th May, 1959 A1 Pacific No. 60148** *Aboyeur* **grabs the attention of passengers on plaform 5 while speeding through with the northbound train. Part of the original GN buildings is visible on the left platform which was converted to an island during the 1930s rebuilding.** (*N.E.Stead collection*)

locomotive depots in and around Doncaster.

The first GN depot was a two-road shed with adjoining fitting shop and turntable on the west flank of the station. But the Doncaster engine fleet soon outgrew this diminutive depot and, following construction of the Decoy and Mineral yards in 1874/75, the big Carr Loco depot was opened in March, 1876.

It came complete with two manual coaling stages and turntables, one at each end of the depot. A separate two-road shed was later added at the south end and leased to the Great Eastern Railway while the L&Y Railway leased No.1 road in the main shed. During the 1930s a mechanical coaling plant was built, followed by a loco turning triangle which for many years replaced the turntables.

But there was another large depot just a stone's throw from Carr. This was Red Bank Lane, a dead-end 'northlight' shed with its own turntable and coal stage. It is reputed to have been owned by the London and North Western Railway which had no lines in or near Doncaster but was leased to the Great Eastern from 1893.

The H&B shed at Bullcroft Junction has been mentioned but another two-road shed at the south west corner of Doncaster station housed the Plant Works pilots. J50 0-6-0Ts could be

seen simmering outside the shed until the mid-1960s.

In 1997 Carr has been the only shed in Doncaster for many years and has no main line allocation, but it is still an important freight diesel depot and train crew signing-on point.

As the years passed, the Doncaster railway scene underwent several notable changes.

The view northwards from the station changed dramatically in 1909/10 when North Bridge carrying the Great North Road replaced a heavily congested level crossing.

In 1938, the station itself was extensively rebuilt. The three through plaforms were increased to four by converting the town side platform into an island. New buildings were added, creating the present layout where the booking hall is isolated from all the platforms which have to be reached by subway.

In 1949 resignalling of the station area saw the old GNR somersault signals replaced by colour lights and six manual boxes - 'A', 'B', South, South Yorkshire, Marshgate and Frenchgate, replaced by new North and South power boxes using a unique sequence switch interlocking system. The old 'C' box continued to control the Plant Works entrance and adjacent yard until the late 1970s.

Operationally, Doncaster station was(and still

The many local passenger trains serving Doncaster had their own attractions, like this one to Cleethorpes via Gainsborough. On this day in April, 1958 it was powered by pioneer D11 4-4-0 No. 62660 *Butler Henderson* while the first two coaches were still in LNER varnished teak. *(Geoff Warnes/Colour-Rail)*

is) a place offering plenty of interest to the observer. In 1959 around 120 departures left its platforms every 24 hours. Practically all ECML expresses either called there or passed through on their way between King's Cross, the North East, Scotland, West Yorkshire and Hull. Their impressive Pacifics were the top attraction, heading such trains as The Flying Scotsman, The Elizabethan, The Queen of Scots and The White Rose. Until the late 1950s, Britain's only 4-6-4 tender locomotive, solitary W1 No. 60700 went into many a notebook. In 1958 an attempt was made to replace the Pacifics with English Electric Type 4(Class 40) diesels but they were no match for the job and steam enjoyed an 'Indian Summer' until the 3,300hp Deltics took over in 1962.

Some trains attached and detached portions at Doncaster, adding to the interest. Most memorable was the Yorkshire Pullman. A Hull B1 4-6-0, K3 2-6-0, D49 4-4-0 or, in later years, English Electric Type 3(Class 37) diesel brought in the four Hull coaches which were attached to the main train, itself a collection of portions from Leeds, Bradford and Harrogate.

Eastern Counties express and stopping trains brought exotic engines from Great Eastern territory. Usual power in the 1950s were B17 Sandringham and Footballer 4-6-0s from March shed, and in the '60s the Britannia Pacifics or perhaps the then rare named Class 37 diesel D6707 *The East Anglian Regiment*.

Local trains too offered plenty of variety until steam was ousted by diesel multiple units. GC engines like D11 4-4-0s, J11 0-6-0s and C13 or C14 4-4-2Ts came in from Sheffield, Barnsley or Cleethorpes. Such North Eastern types as D20 4-4-0s and B16 4-6-0s came from York, Selby

and Hull - for a time some NE engines were outbased at Doncaster. Leeds-Doncaster stopping trains could produce the odd Pacific or Deltic and even ex-LMS engines like Jubilee 4-6-0s towards the end of steam.

More routine but now fading from memory are the GN 0-6-0 tank and tender engines which wandered about on trip, pilot and empty stock workings.

Always entertaining was the Carr wagon works 'Flyer' - a few old wooden coaches and a J52 0-6-0ST which ferried staff between the station and the works.

Special occasions added real spice to the interest but on summer Saturdays many trains to and from the coast used the avoiding line, unseen from the station. The busiest days for specials were race days when many trains used St. James Bridge station which had been retained for that purpose. On St. Leger day thousands of punters once descended on Doncaster in up to a hundred trains and every inch of siding, the Plant Works yard included, was cleared to make room for the empty coaches.

From the 1950s, the works itself attracted special trains hauled by alien locomotives from far away regions, all packed with enthusiasts eager to explore its secrets within.

A steady procession of goods trains, predominantly coal but also iron ore, steel, fish from Hull and Grimsby, and other perishables like fruit and veg from Lincolnshire and East Anglia, passed through the area, again many trains taking the avoiding line or the South Yorkshire Joint. Dominating the heavy goods scene in the 1950s and early 1960s were the ex-GN O2 2-8-0s along with the ex-GC O4s, WDs and Doncaster's own BR Standard 9F 2-10-0s, often so dirty that it was infuriatingly difficult to decipher their numbers. Lighter, faster freights would be in the hands of K3 2-6-0s or J39 0-6-0s while the big ex-LMS Beyer Garratts sneaked round the avoiding line with iron ore from the Midlands to Scunthorpe.

Heavy trains ferried a conveyor belt of coal to the capital's factories and fireplaces. Dubbed the 'Flying Coals', the 900-ton loads left the Up Mineral yard every two hours round the clock for London via Boston and Peterborough. Loose-coupled, they were limited to 35mph and allowed 41 minutes to Gainsborough. Doncaster men worked them to a suitable spot on the Lincoln - Boston line where they swapped with Peterborough men on empties coming the other way. It meant a nine hour shift with no meal break and a round trip of 120 miles. Later the coal was rerouted to the new Whitemoor yard, March, and in 1966 to the Midland Main Line.

Express freights using the GN&GE Joint in the 1960s ran mainly between Whitemoor and such places as Niddrie(Edinburgh), York, Ardsley, Hull and Newcastle. They had to run one after the other in 'flights' to make the most of paths between the endless coal trains. Express freights on the ECML were given top link power, even A4 Pacifics and often V2 2-6-2s which were designed for such work. One of the fastest in the late 1950s was the 8.37pm King's Cross-Hull Class C which ran non-stop from Ferme Park(London) to Belmont Sidings where it arrived at 12.46am after running at an average speed of 42.2mph. Other fast freights passing through first stop York were the Scotch Goods and the Tees-Tyne Freighter.

The presence of the Plant greatly enhanced the variety of locomotives visiting Doncaster with types not otherwise seen there going in and out of works and on running-in turns. In the early 1960s certain withdrawn steam locos came not for scrapping but to be restored for preservation in the national collection. The Plant was also a base for testing new and prototype diesels.

Although freight traffic has reduced considerably since the 1960s, Doncaster has, by the late 1990s at least, managed to escape the kind of total anihilation afflicted on some other railway centres once of similar stature. Only two main lines in the area have closed completely - the Dearne Valley and the H&B and GC Joint.

Apart from the short-lived Worksop service over the South Yorkshire Joint, the first real casualty came in March, 1947 when the Askern branch passenger service was withdrawn and the intermediate stations closed to regular passenger traffic.

The Dearne Valley lost its passenger trains in September, 1951 but the worst loss came on 29th June, 1959 when the Barnsley and Penistone local service was axed. Nearly 40 years on with road congestion and pollution at crisis level, a direct Barnsley - Doncaster link is sorely missed.

Of the remaining local stations, Hampole, on the Leeds Line, was closed to passengers(and goods) on 7th January, 1952; Arksey, on the York line, on 5th August, 1952; Rossington on 6th October, 1958; Finningley, on the Gainsborough line, on 11th September, 1961; Barnby Dun on 4th September, 1967; and Carcroft & Adwick-le-Street on 6th November, 1967. By the time the culling was over, the only local station still handling regular passenger trains was Stainforth and Hatfield. Most of these stations continued to handle goods until the 1960s though goods facilities had already been withdrawn from Barnby Dun and Carcroft by the time they closed to passengers. Another local station in the area was Bramwith, on the WR&G Stainforth-Adwick line. It is not thought to have ever had a regular passenger service but handled goods until 1961.

This line has been the only other to lose its regular passenger service, the direct trains between West Yorkshire and Cleethorpes having been whittled down to just the daily 16.44 Leeds-Cleethorpes by 1979. In 1997 the line was still well used by freight and could accommodate passenger trains if necessary.

Eastern Counties expresses via the GN&GE have also disappeared since the 1970s but infrequent Lincoln and Peterborough local trains remain. Once there were few paths left among the coal trains for a passenger service but by 1997 the line saw hardly any freight at all. In 1990 BR proposed closure of the Doncaster-Gainsborough section but subsequently withdrew the proposal. Services on most other routes have been improved since the 1980s.

The Dearne Valley ceased to be a through route in 1966 but the Doncaster end survived to serve Yorkshire Main Colliery. From 1972 only its connection with the SYJ at St. Catherine's remained after abandonment of the Black Carr West-Bessacarr/Loversall lines.

On the H&B and GC Joint the Doncaster Junction south curve was removed in the 1930s. The line north of Bullcroft Junction shut in October, 1958. The section from Sprotborough to Yorkshire Main Colliery, one line often used for storing crippled wagons, was completely closed by 1969, and Bullcroft Colliery to Doncaster Junction in 1970 leaving only a single track from Sprotborough to York Road via Doncaster Junction North. In 1961 about a mile was reinstated from Bullcroft Jn. to the intersection with the Stainforth-Adwick line for coal trains to Thorpe Marsh power station but was lifted again in 1970 after Thorpe Marsh was connected to the Stainforth-Adwick line.

Freight traffic on most other routes remained heavy until the early 1980s when the Thatcher government set about closing down most of Britain's coal mines. This policy and the bitter 1984/85 miners' strike apposing the pit closures almost finished off the Doncaster coalfield and had a disastrous affect on the railway. Askern, Bentley, Yorkshire Main, Brodsworth, South Kirkby, Hatfield and Markham Main all closed in the years immediately following the strike. Markham Main and Hatfield reopened following the privatisation of British Coal but Markham had closed again by 1996 leaving Hatfield and Rossington the only deep mines in the immediate Doncaster area. The pit closures brought a big reduction in the traffic handled by the yards at Decoy, Hexthorpe and Stainforth, the latter being completely abandoned. Fortunately, coal, steel and petroleum

from South Humberside, the two surviving pits and some others a little further away still generate enough freight through Doncaster to just about hold the observer's interest.

The risk of further service losses looked like being reduced in the 1970s when the South Yorkshire Passenger Transport Executive became responsible for subsidising and co-ordinating public transport in an area covering Sheffield, Barnsley and Doncaster. But for many years, the SYPTE favoured buses and only the Sheffield line into Doncaster received PTE support. The West Yorkshire PTE became similarly responsible in its area, supporting a Leeds-Doncaster stopping service, safeguarding South Elmsall station and reopening Fitzwilliam.

Facing crippling road congestion, South Yorkshire has gradually become more rail-minded. The Sheffield-Doncaster service has been much improved while the PTE has since extended its area of support east of Doncaster, creating more frequent local services to Goole and Scunthorpe, and opening a new station at Kirk Sandall, just on the Doncaster side of the old Barnby Dun station, in 1991. It also opened new stations on the Leeds line at Bentley and

**The awesome sight of four big Pacifics undergoing overhaul in the Crimpsall heavy repair shop at Doncaster works on 23rd May, 1959. From left are BR Standard Britannia No. 70039** *Sir Christopher Wren*, **A3 No. 60107** *Royal Lancer*, **A2 No. 60534** *Irish Elegance* **and A3 No. 60064** *Tagalie*. *(Brian Morrison)*

The railway at Doncaster underwent a radical transformation during the late 1970s rationalisation and resignalling.
Work connected with the scheme was evident at Stainforth and Hatfield on 29th October, 1980 when Brush Type 4 No. 47216 was heading past the station and yard with a westbound train of empty wagons.
*(Derek Porter)*

Adwick, close to the old Carcroft station, and has introduced a Doncaster-Adwick shuttle which turns back on the Carcroft-Skellow curve. The reopenings were designed to cut road congestion, especially on the North Bridge, and hopefully further schemes will follow, perhaps the reopening of Rossington, Askern and Finningley.

The 1970s brought the biggest changes to Doncaster's railway network in 60 years.

In 1974, the Government approved the £25 million Doncaster resignalling. Besides general modernisation and preparation for 125mph High Speed Trains, it reduced the amount of track in line with shrinking freight traffic.

Delayed by economic recession, the work took seven years to complete during which time 52 old signal boxes were replaced by one signalling centre alongside Doncaster station. Using remote interlocking it controlled 73 miles of the East Coast Main Line from south of Grantham to just short of Selby, plus 82 miles of other lines. The complex layout at Black Carr was radically remodelled and the Gainsborough line rerouted over the old Dearne Valley girder bridge clear of the East Coast Main Line. The speed limit for non-stop trains through Doncaster was raised from 60 to 105mph. The last semaphore signal on the ECML, Decoy No.2 Up Home, was ceremonially removed on 27th September, 1978 and the scheme was finally completed in December, 1981.

A decade later came the East Coast Main Line electrification which brought the ECML through Doncaster to where it is in 1997. The scheme, valued at £306 million when authorised by the Government in 1984, involved electrifying the whole route from Hitchin to Edinburgh and Doncaster to Leeds. It included a control room next to Carr Loco depot for monitoring the 25,000 volt power supply while a construction depot for engineers installing the overhead line equipment was set up at Hexthorpe. After the ECML was complete, it supplied engineers and equipment for the Ilkley and Skipton electrification.

The first electric InterCity 225 train to carry passengers from King's Cross to Leeds ran on 3rd March, 1989, and the full electric service on the whole East Coast route was launched in June, 1991 when the massive project, dubbed Britain's longest construction site, was officially declared complete by the Queen.

So far, Doncaster has witnessed five generations of East Coast motive power from the early GNR steam locos and the LNER Pacifics to the powerful Deltics, the InterCity 125s and the 225s capable of 140mph. Hopefully during 1997 they will be joined by Eurostars running direct between Scotland and Paris via the Channel Tunnel, reaching 185mph on the French side.

With these and the opening of the Doncaster Railport, a major international freight terminal built on the Up side at Decoy with the backing of the borough council, Doncaster is becoming a truly European rail centre.

As 1997 dawned the Doncaster railway scene was again undergoing radical change. Railway privatisation meant that all InterCity, mail and most freight trains were no longer run by British Rail and a kalaedoscope of different companies liveries was starting to appear for the first time since the 1920s. Most striking is the deep blue and red of the Great North Eastern Railway which took over all ECML services along with the management of Doncaster station in 1996. Freight trains are headed by locomotives in the maroon and gold of the English, Welsh and Scottish Railway(which took over BR's three trainload freight companies, including Doncaster-based Loadhaul)and by the striking blue American-built Class 59 diesels of National Power.

Coal trains still run through the station and over the South Yorkshire Joint, and steel trains still take the avoiding line but they are fewer nowadays. The EW&S is fighting to win back lost business and recently secured a contract for delivery of house coal to selected depots all over Britain, some of it from Rossington.

A new Royal Mail station was due to open on the site of Down Decoy sidings in 1997, removing mailbag handling from Central station but ensuring that Doncaster remains an important calling point on the postal train network.

Not all the news is so encouraging, and a depressing cycle of decline at the Plant Works begun in the 1980s continues. A decade after the works was broken up into three separate sites, with the loss of 1,800 jobs, the multinational company ADtranz, new owners of the Crimpsall locomotive and multiple unit heavy repair shop, announced that it would be reduced to a skeleton staff with the loss of another 200 jobs by March, 1997. This, said ADtranz, was because most railway operators, EW&S especially, were undertaking heavy maintenance at their own depots.

The former diesel multiple unit repair shop continues as a national supply centre for rolling stock spares distributed to depots all over the country by lorry. The rest of the Plant, including the wagon shops and new build erecting shop, has despite one or two closure scares, continued as a railway works since being sold to RFS Industries in 1987, though the chances of new main line locomotives ever being built in Doncaster again seem very very remote.

**The Plant Works attracted trainloads of enthusiasts eager to see what went on behind its normally closed doors.**
**Here, the Plant's most famous product, A3 Pacific No. 60103** *Flying Scotsman* **sets off for home via Sheffield with an Ian Allan Locospotters Club special.** *(Derek Porter)*

**Above: Deltic No. D9001** *St. Paddy* **slows into the 60mph slack that it will face all the way to Bentley Colliery while passing the closed Rossington station with a northbound express from King's Cross on 1st January, 1964.** *(Derek Porter)*

**Back in 1946, Rossington had a paltry service by any standard. The 7.32am Doncaster-Peterborough via Newark, Sleaford and Spalding called there at 7.52; the 4.55pm all stations Doncaster - Peterborough at 5.4pm; the 6.44am Grantham to York called there at 7.54 on Saturdays, and the 1.10pm Grantham to Doncaster at 2.51.**

**Besides what few passengers there must have been, the Handbook of Stations showed Rossington as being equipped to handle "parcels, miscellaneous traffic, furniture vans, carriages, motor cars, portable engines, machines on wheels, livestock, horse boxes and prize cattle vans, and carriages and motor cars by passenger or parcels trains." Goods facilities were withdrawn on 27th May, 1963.**

# EIGHT MILES OF MAIN LINE MAGIC

Just north of Rossington, the maximum speed on the ECML Main and Fast lines in the 1960s dropped from 70 to 60mph and the restriction was in force for eight miles to Bentley Colliery where the speed then rose to 80mph.

There were signal boxes at Rossington, Loversall Carr, Black Carr Jn., Potterick Carr, Decoy No. 1 Down, Decoy No. 2 Up, Red Bank, Balby Jn., Bridge Jn., Doncaster South, Doncaster North, Arksey, Bentley Colliery, and Shaftholme Jn. There were also goods boxes at Decoy(Pointsman's box), Carr(controlling goods and engine lines only), and Sand Bank(goods, Up and Down Transfer lines only), and Doncaster 'C'.

Absolute Block signalling was in force on the Up and Down Main lines with Permissive Block between Doncaster South and North. Track Circuit Block was later introduced on the Down Main between Doncaster North and Arksey.

Up and Down Goods lines were provided throughout from Rossington to Doncaster South with additional lines at many places, especially between Potterick Carr and Bridge Jn. Two Up and Two Down Slow lines were provided between Doncaster South and North along with two additional Down Goods lines, and two further Down Goods lines between 'C' Box and Doncaster North.

All Goods lines were Permissive Block but there was no block on the additional goods line between Red Bank and Carr, the Up Goods lines between Bridge Jn. and Doncaster South, Bridge Jn. and Doncaster North, and all the Down Goods lines between Doncaster South and North.

*The East Coast Main Line between Rossington and Bawtry was bordered by Bawtry Forest which could be a serious fire hazard in dry weather. Drivers were warned to take special care to avoid the emission of sparks and cinders in this area, especially between February and May.*

14

Above: A historic moment on New Year's Day, 1964 when *Flying Scotsman* made its first run in preservation, a test run to Barkeston Junction(north of Grantham) and back following overhaul at the Plant and repainting in LNER pre-war livery. No. 4472 was photographed approaching Potterick Carr on the outward run. *(Derek Porter)*

The 1960 Eastern Region Sectional Appendix stated that up to 60 wagons could be worked without a brake van at the rear on all Down Goods lines between Doncaster Decoy No. 1 and Doncaster North, on the Up Fast Goods, Up Slow Goods, Up Reception No.1 and Up Departure No.2 lines between Decoy No.2 Up and Potterick Carr, on all Goods lines between Doncaster South and Decoy No.2, and across all main lines at Doncaster yards.

Below: BR  Standard Britannia Pacific No.70009 *Alfred The Great* displays Through Freight headlamps while hauling a 204hp diesel  shunter and English Electric Type 4 No. D285 past Decoy yards in the direction of  Doncaster in the early 1960s. This picture is looking towards Potterick Carr and was taken from a footbridge leading to the  Carr  wagon works. *(Derek Porter)*
Decoy yards are reputed to have got their name from the decoy ducks used by hunters on the marshes which surround the area. and which are now a nature reserve.

Situated at a remote spot called Spike Island, Carr wagon works comprised a seven-road North Shop which built new wagons, and a 15-road South Shop where wagons were repaired. There was also a paint shop and a large stockyard for timber, the main material for wagons in those days.

The North shop could accommodate around 140 wagons and the South shop around 220.

Among vehicles built there during GNR days were open wagons, brake vans, gas cylinder wagons, horse boxes, fish vans and breakdown cranes. After formation of the LNER in 1923, Carr works concentrated mainly on repairs.

Under the 1960s British Railways workshops review, the wagon works was returned to the Plant, taking the place of carriage shops made vacant by the end of carriage building and classified repairs there.

In 1997 the Carr buildings were used by private industry.

**Above: Wagons did not always enter and leave the Carr Works by their own wheels. This body from a crippled standard BR 16-ton mineral wagon had arrived firmly secured to a Lowmac wagon.** *(Derek Porter)*

**Below: An official BR photograph showing part of the Carr Wagon Works timber yard in 1948.** *(Derek Porter collection)*

DECOY UP AND DOWN YARDS - All Down mixed trains of goods and empties must be marshalled as follows: - empty coal wagons next to engine, goods and foreign empties next to brake van. *Eastern Region Sectional Appendix, October 1960.*

WD 2-8-0 No. 90138 was a Lancashire engine from Rose Grove, Burnley, and was probably preparing to head for home via Knottingley, Wakefield and the Calder Valley with this Through Freight from Decoy Down sidings early in 1963. The first vehicle is another WD, dead and covered in snow. *(Derek Porter)*

Derek Porter began work as an apprentice fitter at the Carr wagon works in July, 1949 when his first job was operating the steam hammer, making axle guards and 'through bars' for wooden framed wagons.

"Sometimes I went with a fitter to Pilkington's sidings at Kirk Sandall to do minor repairs on the glass carrying wagons, fitting new chains and repairing screws. On the way I once saw a J52 on the Wheatley Park trading estate line.

"Carr works was in two parts. The north shop did heavy repairs while the south shop did light repairs and I repaired the doors on containers there, down at the end where they had the grease factories. Two Sentinel steam locos shunted the yard.

"Very occasionally we had to walk across the main lines to collect spares from Bells wagon works in the old Red Bank engine shed.

"They did all private owner wagons there and I think they had a small industrial loco.

"The old shed was just as it was when it closed but without a turntable or coaling stage. I think it had eleven roads."

Although he lived nearby in Balby, Derek Porter caught the bus into town so that he could ride to work on the staff train which shuttled between the station and the Carr works

"I did it for the fun of it. It was a set of articulated coaches pulled by a J52 or J50 but sometimes a K3 or a B1, and at least once a V2.

"It's official nickname was the 'Spike Island Flyer' but we also called it the 'Flying Flea.' It ran to a wooden platform which was connected to the works by a footbridge across the goods lines at Down Decoy.

"As a youngster I often went to Slacks's tip, near Balby bridge. One day in August, 1947, as I walked there down Balby Road I heard a big bang and when I got to the railway I found terrible carnage. A V2 had gone into the back of an express. I don't remember how many, but I know a lot of people were killed. The thing that sticks in my mind most is seeing an undamaged push-chair being taken from the guard's van.

"After school we would go to see repaired locos coming out of the Plant and at 4.30 the O1s and L1s going through on their way to Darlington works and the O2s to Cowlairs."

When Carr works was closing Derek Porter was one of the first men transferred to the new wagon works at the Plant.

"The place was just an empty shell when we arrived. I looked round and in the paint store I found the headboard from King George the Sixth's funeral train. I nearly bought it, the price was 12 shillings and sixpence (62.5p).

"I well remember all the locos being cut up, the nameplates and works plates just lying around the storeyard. What they couldn't sell they smashed up with hammers. In 1962 I bought the name and works plates from the A1/1 *Great Northern* for £17.50.

"Another memorable time was in 1982, after the Deltics were withdrawn and we had them at the Plant for scrapping. We were under siege with people breaking in to see them. We lined them up so that they could see them from outside and persuaded the works manager to hold an open day for a last look at the Deltics in the hope that after that the enthusiasts would leave us alone. It was a great success and the proceeds went to charity."

Derek Porter played a key role in organising the Doncaster works open days which attracted thousands of visitors from all over the country.

Left: Derek Porter was in the right spot to get this photo of V2 2-6-2 No. 60871 being rerailed by Doncaster's 45-ton breakdown crane in 1963. He was just crossing the footbridge to Carr wagon shops on his way to work when the loco came off the rails while hauling a Down goods train right underneath him.

The wagon works sidings are on the left, Decoy goods lines stretch ahead to Doncaster and the East Coast Main Line is to the right.

Down below on the right, the train which brought Carr wagon shops workers from Doncaster to their day's labour is standing at the wooden platform from where they crossed the footbridge to reach the works.

In the distance, running left to right, are the remains of Red Bank viaduct, closed by Act of Parliament in 1922.

Below: As yet un-named, Deltic No. D9008, later *The Green Howards*, travels past Decoy yards at 60mph with the 10.25am Newcastle to King's Cross in 1963.
*(Derek Porter)*

Doncaster Carr and Red Bank as it was in the early 1950s. The Up(loaded) and Down (empty)Mineral yards and Carr loco depot fill the centre of the picture. The old Red Bank engine shed, by then used as wagon repair shops, is on the extreme right. Prominent at Carr depot are the white-roofed loco repair shop right of the running shed, and the coaling plant with one of the old coaling stages above right of it and fuel tanks for oil firing to the right. The Up Goods lines and Sand Bank yard are to the left of the coaler. Right of the loco shed is the engine turning triangle. Bottom left of the picture is the Carr wagon works timber yard and, bottom right, Red Bank gas works with gas cylinder wagons used for taking gas to outlying stations where it was used for lighting and heating. *(Aerofilms)*

**Above:** The O2 2-8-0s designed by Sir Nigel Gresley and built at Doncaster from 1921 were a familiar sight on goods trains around Doncaster until their withdrawal from traffic between 1962 and 63. Then Mexborough-based No. 63977, one of the Class O2/3s introduced in 1932 with a side window cab and lower pitched boiler, was leading empty coal wagons behind Balby Junction signal box and into the Up Bank mineral sidings on 31st Augst, 1954. *(Brian Morrison)*

UP BANK YARD: Guards working trains onto the Up Bank must.....inform the Poinstman.....what train they have worked in and the number of empty wagons which it conveyed.
Locomotives from Doncaster Bank Reception Roads to Carr Loco must proceed through No.1 Siding to the south end of the yard. A Stop board is provided at the south end of No.1 Siding at ground level, situated between No.1 Siding and the Up Main line, and worded "Drivers must not pass this board without the authority of the shunter." *Addition to the Eastern Region Sectional Appendix, 1960.*

**Below:** One of Sir Nigel Gresley's more glamorous Doncaster products. The world"s fastest steam locomotive, Class A4 Pacific No. 60022 *Mallard* passes Balby Junction box while gathering speed with a Leeds/Bradford to King's Cross express on 31st August, 1954. The inverted headboard is being returned to London for the next day's White Rose back to Leeds. *(Brian Morrison)*

**8.9.57:** BR Class 5 4-6-0 73162 and V2 2-6-2 60918 leave Doncaster double-heading the York-Yarmouth express. On the 14th it is 73162 and B1 4-6-0 61021 *Reitbok*.

**19.10.57:** A3s 60102 *Sir Frederick Banbury*, 60104 *Solario*, A1/1 60113 *Great Northern*, A1 60114 *W.P.Allen* and B1s 61009 *Hartebeeste* and 61152 all transferred to Doncaster.

**19 & 20.9.58:** W1 4-6-4 60700 works the 6.40am local to Sheffield Victoria, returning light engine.

**22.11.58:** Midland 1P 0-4-4T 58085 from Newark is dead on Doncaster shed.

Above: An imposing view of ex-works K1 2-6-0 No. 62022, also on 31st August, 1954. It was passing Balby Junction and setting off for its home depot at Blaydon, on Tyneside, with a Decoy to Newcastle goods following overhaul at the Plant.
Carr Loco depot is on the left and the exit from the Down Mineral yard(Belmont) on the right. *(Brian Morrison)*

Below: An ensemble of Cravens(Class 105) and Metro-Cammell (Class 101) DMUs take an interesting route past Carr Loco depot with a returning special from the 1981 Finningley air show.. The 1970s rationalisation has clearly left its mark.
*(Derek Porter)*

**Above: One of the rare visitors which from time to time found their way to Doncaster with enthusiasts' specials. Southern Region West Country Pacific No. 34094 *Mortehoe* rests on Doncaster Carr shed in company with an A4, a B16 4-6-0 and a 9F 2-10-0 after bringing a railtour from Birmingham on 12th May, 1963.** (*Derek Porter*)

Doncaster Carr motive power depot comprised a 12-road running shed capable of housing 100 locomotives, a two road heavy repair shop and a large administrative block. A magnificent four-face clocktower with 6ft dials once stood on the west side of the shed. Improvements in the 1930s included the mechanical coaling plant, wet ash pits and a turning triangle. During the 1950s the running shed was rebuilt and the hipped, tiled roof replaced by concrete beams and glazing. In 1960 a 70ft turntable was installed at the north end and the triangle abandoned.

In BR days the 36A shedcode fired the imagination of youthful spotters everywhere and meant a wide variety of interesting engines ranging from famous Pacifics to pre-grouping 2-8-0s.

For its crews, moving millions upon millions of tons of coal to London was the main task but they were also rostered for the elite top link passenger turns. Famous expresses worked by Doncaster men over the years include The Scarborough Flyer, The Yorkshire Pullman, The White Rose, The Aberdonian, The Hull Pullman, The Bradford Executive and The South Yorkshireman between Leicester Central and Nottingham Victoria.

Carr Loco, as it is known locally, closed to steam in April, 1966, the last steam shed in the old Eastern Region of BR, but still provided water for visiting engines on short stopovers. With the end of steam, Doncaster's allocation of main line locomotives, once around 200, was wiped out. Throughout the diesel era, its only allocation has been shunters but it has continued to be a servicing outbase for main line locomotives allocated to Immingham and a good selection of freight engines, including Classes 31, 37, 47, 56, 58 and 60 could still be seen there in 1997.

## LOCOMOTIVES ALLOCATED TO DONCASTER  September, 1961

A1/1 4-6-2: 60113 *Great Northern*; A1 4-6-2: 60114 *W.P.Allen*/ 60119 *Patrick Stirling* / 60122 *Curlew*/ 60125 *Scottish Union*/ 60128 *Bongrace*/ 60136 *Alcazar*/ 60139 *Sea Eagle*/ 60144 *King's Courier*/ 60149 *Amadis*/60156 *Great Central*/60157 *Great Eastern*/60158 *Aberdonian*; A2/3 4-6-2: 60520 *Owen Tudor*/60523 *Sun Castle*; A2 4-6-2: 60533 *Happy Knight*; V2 2-6-2: 60826/ 49/ 50/ 2/7 66/70/60872 *King's Own Yorkshire Light Infantry*/75/80/9/96/9/908/9/12/7/28 /30/ 5/6/43; B1 4-6-0: 61001 *Eland*/ 61003*Gazelle*/ 61036 *Ralph Assheton* /55/87/1107/21/2/4/5/7/8/35/45/57/8/70/93/6/ 61250 *A. Harold Bibby*/70/9/1314/26/60/5; K3 2-6-0: 61800/3/12/29/39/50/67/8/82/95/1925/40/61/4; K1 2-6-0: 62036/53; O4 2-8-0: 63613/8/93/8/858; O2 2-8-0: 63922/8/35/41/62/7/8/74/7/8/81/4/5;  L1 2-6-4T: 67780/4/7; J50 0-6-0T: 10/11(works shunters)/ 68962/3/4/5/77; WD 2-8-0: 90001/63/ 79/144/ 235/55/86/96/453/76/96/8/506/38/51/69/636/83/709; 9F 2-10-0: 92168-77/89/90/1/2/8/9/2200/1; 350hp 0-6-0 diesel: D3439/43/4/73/4/9/80/1/2/3/4/621/2/3/37/48/9/50/1, Total: 164.

**Above:** The steam age in all its glory. Amid a carpet of oil and wet cinders outside the Carr running shed , the fireman of King's Cross A3 No. 60039 *Sandwich* oils round before returning south. *(Derek Porter)*

**Below:** When the turntable was reinstated at the North end of Carr Loco in 1960, on the site of the fuel oil tanks, the turning triangle was removed to make room for the 'Woodyard' engineers' sidings. *Mortehoe* makes use of the new turntable during its stopover with the Warwickshire Railway Society special of 12th May, 1963. The turntable was decommissioned in April, 1966. *(Derek Porter).*

Old and new coaling plants at Carr depot.

Left: The new mechanical coaler shortly after construction in the 1930s with LNER A1 Pacific No. 2543 *Melton* (later rebuilt as A3) being replenished. The reinforced concrete structure proved extremely difficult to demolish following the end of steam. *(Official LNER photograph/Derek Porter collection)*

Below: The old ramped coaling stage at the north end of the shed, where coal was loaded by hand on to the engines, survived many years after the new plant was commissioned. Two North Eastern visitors, B16/3 4-6-0s Nos. 61439 and 61468 were resting alongside on 12th April, 1959.
*(Neville Stead)*

No. 60700 was built at Darlington in 1930 as LNER No. 10000, an experimental 4-cylider compound with a Yarrow-Gresley water tube boiler working at a pressure of 450lb per square inch.

It was the first streamlined locomotive in Britain but looked very different to 60700 and was nicknamed the 'Hush Hush' because it was built in great secrecy.

Fitted with a corridor tender, No. 10000 worked such expresses as The Queen of Scots and The Flying Scotsman.

Failing to achieve the fuel economy which Gresley had hoped for and proving expensive to maintain, it was rebuilt along the lines of an A4 Pacific in 1937, the high pressure boiler being replaced by a conventional one, the compound motion changed to 3-cylinder simple, and A4-style streamlining fitted. The most powerful high-speed streamlined loco in Britain, it was withdrawn in June, 1959.

**Above: One of the more unusual engines on Doncaster's books, the sole W1 4-6-4 No. 60700 hides inside the shed while receiving attention from the fitters on 31st August, 1954.**
*(Brian Morrison)*

**Below: By the late 1950s, the elderly ex-GN J52 0-6-0STs were fast disappearing from local pilot work leaving a shortage of shunting engines to work alongside the J50 tanks. Temporary replacements had to be drafted in to bridge the gap and they included ex-Great Eastern J68 0-6-0T No. 68654 and two J69s(68502 the in the middle), standing at the north end of the shed on 24th May, 1959.** *(Neville Stead)*

A 45 ton steam breakdown crane, No. 330107, was stationed at Doncaster Carr depot in the 1960s.

Its area reached to, *Gainsborough, Newark, Misson, Edlington, Laughton East on the South Yorkshire Joint, Warmsworth on the H&B and GC Joint, Hemsworth, Crowle, Thorne North, Thorpe Marsh power station, and Knottingley. It could also be called to serious blockages at Scunthorpe, Worksop and Grantham, and was available to assist in emergency as far away as Leeds, Hull and Normanton.*

*It travelled at 45mph and had a route availability of 9 which could be eased to 7 with a 15mph restriction.*

**Above: Just about anything could turn up at Doncaster, it seems. This rare bird, ex-Midland 2F 0-6-0T No. 41779 was sharing the ash pit with more usual J50 0-6-0T No. 68974 at 1.37pm on 2nd December, 1956.** *(David Holmes)*

**Below: Stood by the breakdown train on the same day was even more appetising ex-Midland 1P 0-4-4T No. 58085 bearing a 36F shedplate. No. 58085 was probably visiting Doncaster shed for heavy maintenance or boiler washout.** *(David Holmes)*

Tanks on shed at Carr Loco.
**Right:** Ex-GNR J52 0-6-0STs did much of the shunting work around Doncaster until the late 1950s. No. 68836 was inactive in the shed yard on 29th September, 1956.
*(David Holmes)*

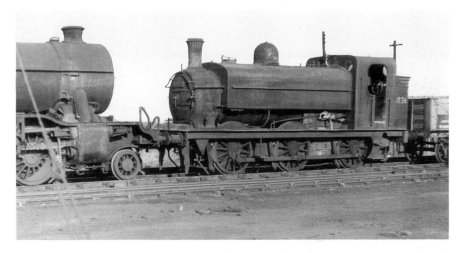

**Left:** Rebuilding of the shed roof was hopefully not too far away when King's Cross N2 0-6-2T No. 69591 was stood outside on 2nd December, 1956. 69591 was one of those equipped with condensing gear for working on the London underground Metropolitan widened lines to Moorgate.
*(David Holmes)*

**Right:** In 1960 Doncaster was sent three L1 2-6-4Ts for pilot and trip work. No. 67780 was one and stands cold outside the rebuilt shed with K1 2-6-0 No. 62069 and B1 4-6-0 No. 61158.
*(Derek Porter)*

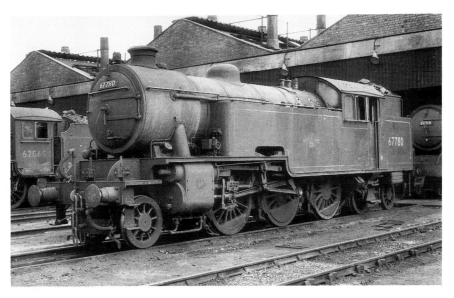

On 8th November, 1960 Peter Rose logged 62 steam locomotives on Doncaster shed. They were Doncaster-based A1/1 60113; A1s 60128/36/39/44/56; A2/3 60520; V2s 60817/26/49/52/75/89/905/36/43; B1s 61087/ 1128/ 45/70/93; K3s 61925/40; O4s 63677/93/8/858; O2s 63958/ 62/81; J39s 64810/74/ 987; J94 0-6-0STs 68020/69/71; J69 68508 J50 68962; WDs 90144/296/551; 9Fs 92171/6/99/201.

Visiting engines were: 5P5F 2-6-0 42794(41B); 8F 2-8-0 48440(2E); A4 60011(64B); A3 60064(34F); V2 60941 (50A); B1s 61188(40E) 61211(36E)/61295(56B); K3 61807(40A); K1s 62033(31B) 62048/58(51A); O4 63576 (36C); O2s 63925/34(36E); WD 90422 (36C).

**Above:** Beneath the concrete beamed roof of the rebuilt shed, O4/8 2-8-0 No. 63823, a visitor from Ardsley, receives attention to its cylinders. No. 63823 was one of the batch rebuilt from 1944 onwards with the standard LNER 100A boiler but keeping its original cylinders. *(Derek Porter)*

**Below:** Alongside the ashpits by the old north end coaling stage on 19th March, 1961 were J50 0-6-0T No. 68965, A2 Pacific No. 60536 *Trimbush*, and an O2 2-8-0. Wagons loaded with timber fill the Up Bank yard. *(Peter Rose)*

The driver of J39/1 0-6-0 No. 64721 looks as though he means business as his train thunders over Bridge Junction with a northbound train of perishables on 31st August, 1954. Situated under Balby Road bridge, Bridge Junction is the point where the south curve to St. James Junction and the Mexborough line leaves the East Coast Main Line. *(Brian Morrison)*

Friday 16th March, 1951 was a black day, for on that day 14 people died in a horrific accident which befell the 10.6am to King's Cross.

The express, 14 coaches with a horse box on the rear and hauled by A2/2 Pacific No. 60501 *Cock O' the North*, had left platform 4 and was taking the Up Slow to Up Main scissors crossover at Bridge Junction when it left the rails.

No. 60501 and the first two coaches stayed on the track but the next eight were derailed. The third coach swung through 90 degrees and was crushed to destruction against the pier of Balby bridge. All the dead were in this coach.

Another 29 passengers were injured and all the derailed coaches damaged. The Main and Slow lines were blocked for 13 hours and the two Up Goods lines until 5pm on Sunday. Doncaster, York and Peterborough cranes were needed and ECML trains diverted via Darnall and Retford.

The subsequent accident report by Railway Inspecting Officers Lt.-Col. G.R.S. Wilson and Brigadier C.A. Langley also gave an interesting insight into operations at Doncaster.

It revealed that there were on average 42 movements a day from the Up Slow to the Up Main and 94 along the Up Main, including many through expresses travelling up to 60mph. The Up Slow from the platform to Bridge Jn. was subject to a 10mph speed restriction because of a steep rise in the cant(the way the track leans into a curve) at the trailing end of the crossover.

The first six coaches of the train were the 8.45 am from Hull and the rest were the 9.15am from York which had combined at Doncaster.

Nine coaches, including the third, had steel panelled bodies on hardwood frames, the rest were all timber. No. 60501 had just had an intermediate overhaul at Doncaster works.

The train's departure was described: "...the 0-6-0 tank engine, which had attached the York portion at the rear, assisted by pushing for one or two coach lengths....The station master, Mr. J. E. Fisher, said it was usual to assist the start when an Up express was formed at platform 4."

On 11th April three special runpasts with 60501 and 14 coaches were used to gauge the speed of the derailed train. Earlier checks by civil engineers found that an A4 with 14 coaches attained 23mph by the time the engine reached Bridge Jn. and an A1 15mph.

The inspecting officers ultimately concluded that the derailment was caused by the failure of a wing rail in a crossing at the crossover.

They criticised drivers for routinely exceeding the 10mph speed limit and deduced that 60501 was doing 20-25mph but added this was not the major cause of the accident. Track maintenance standards were also criticised.

Most locomotives did not have speedometers then and they said such apparatus should be fitted to all the new BR Standard engines and to all locos likely to work express passenger trains. The report also called for a study into the behaviour of the bolts holding crossings together.

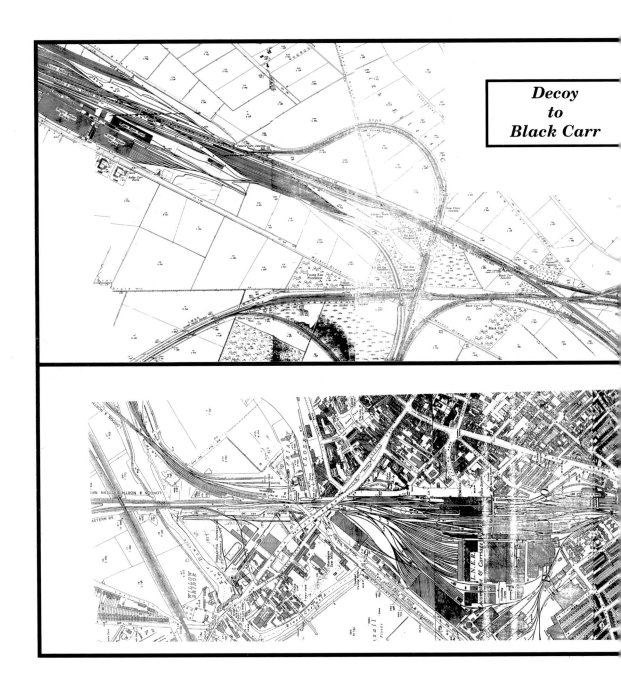

Trains must not be left on the Reception or Slow Goods lines in Decoy Up and Down yards without a flag or tail lamp being placed on the last vehicle by day, and a tail lamp by night. Flags and tail lamps are kept in Decoy yards for this purpose..... *Eastern Region Sectional Appendix, 1968*

**The railway from Black Carr Junction to Marshgate in 1935 as reproduced from a 1 in 2500 Ordnance Survey map.** *By courtesy of the Ordnance Survey*

*Marshgate to Decoy*

In 1968, the 484-yard single track from Black Carr Sidings East to Rossington Colliery was worked under One Engine in Steam regulations with a maximum speed of 15mph. A token was used in lieu of a train staff, there being a post for delivering and receiving the token at Black Carr Sidings East Jn.

Above: As the steam era drew to a close, some exotic visitors reached Doncaster on railtours. A Home Counties Railway Society outing on 9th June, 1963 brought Stanier Coronation Pacific No. 46245 *City of London* to the East Coast Main Line. Having just passed under Hexthorpe Road bridge, it is seen heading towards Bridge Junction with the return run to London. *(Neville Stead)*

Below: The Bridge Junction area in March 1978 with Deltic No. 55012 *Crepello* passing Garden Sidings on the approach to the station with a northbound Inter-City service. Resignalling has not yet eliminated Bridge Junction signal box which is still situated by the rear of the train. The goods dock on the left is packed with tractors, loaded there since closure of the line to Wheatley Park industrial estate and the International Harvesters factory in 1971. ( *Derek Porter*)

Staple traffic at Doncaster.

Above: W1 4-6-4 No. 60700 nears journey's end with a King's Cross to Doncaster service on Saturday 8th July, 1955. The goods yard on the left was doing good business in the days when the railways were common carriers which meant they had to take everything offered to them. The large rectangular building displays the legend 'Whitworth's Ales'. Garden Sidings on the right are full of engines on empty coaching stock. *(Geoff Warnes)*

Below: It is said that all the coal mined in South Yorkshire was taken to London by the Great Northern Railway which actually bought the coal and sold it on to London merchants at a profit. In BR days a train of returning empties on its way from the Down Mineral yard to one of the pits north of Doncaster is brought slowly along the Down Goods past Garden Sidings by Doncaster Class O2/3 2-8-0 No. 63981. *(N.E.Stead collection)*

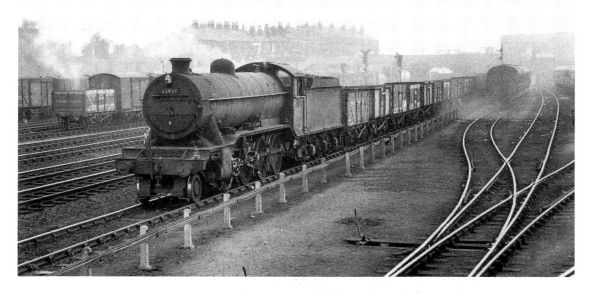

Hexthorpe Road bridge provided photographers with a great vantage point until the overhead wires went up in the 1980s, overlooking as it did the station and the Plant Works entrance. The next few pictures capture some of the delightful scenes which could be enjoyed there.
Above: A4 Pacific No. 60012 *Commonwealth of Australia* races south with a non-stop express in 1958. A V2 waits on stand-by in case of an engine failure. *(Peter Cookson collection)*.

Below: With trackwork under way at Doncaster South in the early 1960s, filthy B1 4-6-0 No. 61047 sets off from the station with a returning summer Saturday excursion from the coast. In the left background can be seen the Plant Works engine shed with a J50 pilot alongside. *(Derek Porter)*

When the GNR set up the Carr wagon works hundreds of workers were transferred from the Plant to the remote Spike Island site so the company provided them with a shuttle train from Doncaster.

Known as "The Spike Island Flyer" it carried express headlamps and ran non-stop between the works and the main line station.

Everyone on the station platform had to watch out when the Flyer came in as the doors would be flying open and its passengers leaping out. The train was already empty by the time it stopped.

It once consisted of 13 GNR 4-wheelers, one 6-wheeler and a J52 0-6-0ST crewed by wagon works locomen who shunted the works yard during the day.

**Above: J52 0-6-0ST No. 68853 approaches the station at teatime on 25th September, 1954 with the "Spike Island Flyer", composed on this occasion of elderly departmental bogie coaches.** (*Geoff Warnes*)

**Below: Another variety of locomotive to be seen at Doncaster. After working in a train from the North Eastern Region, Bridlington D49/1 4-4-0 No. 62701 *Derbyshire* leaves the station with empty coaching stock in August, 1959.** (*Geoff Warnes / Colour-Rail*)

In post-war 1946, 19 expresses left Doncaster for London every 24 hours. Most were from Leeds and Bradford or Hull while two sleeper trains from Newcastle, one from Edinburgh, and the Aberdonian called there in the early hours. Only one daytime train from Scotland, and one from Newcastle, called there. Daytime trains took between 3 and 3.5 hours to reach London but fastest was the 12.10pm Harrogate-King's Cross which got there in 3hr 2 min having travelled to Doncaster via Church Fenton and Knottingley.

**Above: With the Plant Works as a rambling backdrop, Mexborough B1 4-6-0 No. 61093 manoeuvres coaches at the south end of the station in 1961. Through the smoke can be seen the Plant Works engine shed while Doncaster South signal box is visible above the last coach.**

**Below: Doncaster's own V2 2-6-2 No. 60899 was in such excellant condition that it was probably ex-works when captured stood alongside the goods depot.** *(Both Derek Porter)*

*The 1957 Handbook of Stations showed Doncaster Central Goods as being equipped with a 7 ton crane and able to handle "furniture vans, carriages, motor cars, portable engines, machines on wheels and livestock."*

Above: A gloriously steamy scene during the 1960s realignment of South Junction. B1 61170 is on an engineers' train, ex-LMS Black Five 4-6-0 No. 44896 from Farnley Junction waits alongside, and an A3 approaches the gang of men stood perilously close to the Fast line. *(Derek Porter)*

Below: A dozen or so years later the Plant, its offices stretching into the distance, is owned by British Rail Engineering Ltd., the works engine shed has gone, and the goods sidings(right) have been lifted to make way for the new power signal box. The date is 22nd March, 1975 and Class 40 No. 40016 *Campania* is the power for an express freight on the Up Slow line. Class 40s began working freights all the way from Millerhill yard(Edinburgh) to Whitemoor and back in 1963. Between outward and return journeys they also managed to fit in a return Whitemoor-Doncaster trip. *(Adrian Booth)*

Above: One of Doncaster's vintage J6 0-6-0s, No. 64232, trundles a fascinatingly mixed trip working, possibly from Marshgate to Decoy, along the Up Goods line during the 1950s. The standby loco is A1 Pacific No. 60161 *North British*. Being an Edinburgh Haymarket engine, it may well have just come out of the works.

Below: Another classic 0-6-0 but about 15 years younger, was J39/1 No. 64712 which was heading an evening stopping train to Lincoln on 11th September, 1954. *(Both N.E.Stead collection)*

Above: More exotic visitors on railtour duty. Great Western 4-4-0 No. 3440 *City of Truro* and ex-Midland Railway Compound 4-4-0 No. 1000, both restored by BR for working special trains, head south with the return working of an Ian Allan Locospotters Club special in April, 1960. (*Derek Porter*)


Below: A glorious summer evening in 1961 and the glorious sight of another "Streak". Immaculate 60029 *Woodcock* passes Doncaster South box on its way into the station with an express from King's Cross which will divide into separate portions for York and Hull. (*Peter Cookson*)

Above Class A1 Pacific No. 60133 *Pommern* passes the station at 60mph with a Pullman train bound for London in the late 1950s *(Derek Porter)*

Below: A wonderfully panoramic view of the platforms at the south end of Doncaster Central station seen from the footbridge leading to the works on 23rd May, 1959. B16/3 4-6-0 No. 61464 arrives at platform 5 with an express for York, a gas wagon lurks in the bay on the extreme right while St. James's church dominates the whole scene. *(Brian Morrison)*

## SHORT MEMORIES

**April, 1959**: A1 4-6-2s 60122/8/36/9/56/7 transferred from King's Cross to Doncaster.

**12.7.59**: Ardsley K1 2-6-0s 62005/9 and B16 61440 noted hauling West Riding to Cleethorpes excursions over the Adwick-Stainforth line. D11 4-4-0s 62667 *Somme* and 62670 *Marne* pass through the Doncaster area with excursions from Sheffield while 5P5F 2-6-0 42703 of Manchester Newton Heath is also on a Cleethorpes working.

Above: One of the delights of train watching at Doncaster was that Pacifics could be closely observed passing at speed, like A3 No. 60039 *Sandwich* on an Up express in the early 1960s. Nowadays, InterCity 225s whiz past so fast that if you blink you miss them. *(Neville Stead)*

Below: Viewed from the works footbridge in the above picture on 24th April, 1957, V2 2-6-2 No. 60917 waits the "Right Away" from platform 4 with a southbound express. *(N.E.Stead collection)*

**Above:** One of the highlights of a day at Doncaster in the 1950s was the appearance of a B17 4-6-0 from the Eastern Counties. Normally *Gayton Hall, Milton or Gilwell Park*, it arrived in the late morning and returned south around teatime. On this occasion it was No. 61630 *Tottenham Hotspur* awaiting departure from platform 2. (*N.E.Stead collection*)

**Below:** After the B17s came the BR Standard Britannia Pacifics based at March. No. 70034 *Thomas Hardy* waits at plaform 4 with an Eastern Counties train in 1961. (*Derek Porter*)

On Mondays to Fridays in summer, 1963 the only booked passenger trains between the GN&GE Joint and Doncaster were the York-Lowestoft and Newcastle-Colchester, expresses plus one local, the 5.55am to Lincoln. Several parcels trains ran in the evening and early hours. A test train path was the 8.15am to Lincoln Holmes yard and 11.5 return.

On Saturdays, though, there were alsotrains to Skegness(4), Yarmouth (2) and 8 return workings, plus the 8.18am to Mablethorpe and 11.40 return, the 9.12 Lincoln -Blackpool and 10.45 return, and a 7.35pm DMU to Lincoln.

# Principal services from Doncaster  Summer, 1959

**am**

| | | |
|---|---|---|
| 1.04 | Dundee | *Sleeper from King's Cross* |
| 3.17 | Cleethorpes. | *From Manchester* |
| 3.35 | Newcastle | *From King's Cross* |
| 3.47 MO | Newcastle | *From King's Cross* |
| 4.26 | Selby, York | *From King's Cross* |
| 4.43 | Hull | *From King's Cross* |
| 8.6 | Leeds/Bradford | *From King's Cross* |
| 8.29 | Bridlington | *From 22nd June* |
| 8.45 | Cleethorpes | *From 22nd June* |
| 10.53 | Brad ford/Leeds | *From King's Cross* |
| 11.5 | Hull | *From King's Cross/Sheffield* |
| 11.45 | Leeds/Bradford | *The White Rose* |

**pm**

| | | |
|---|---|---|
| 12.36 | Hull | *From Liverpool Central* |
| 12.48 | Newcastle | *From Colchester* |
| 1.15 FO | Edinburgh | *From Peterborough 23/7 - 28/8* |
| 1.18 MO | Leeds/Bradford | *From King's Cross* |
| 1.38 | Leeds/Bradford, Ripon | *From K. Cross* |
| 1.44 | Hull | *From King's Cross* |
| 3.31 | Newcastle | *From Yarmouth 16/7 - 28/8* |
| 3.31 | York | *From Yarmouth/Lowestoft 3rd July, 4th and 11th September* |
| 4.10 MFO | Leeds/Bradford | *From King's Cross* |
| 4.21 | Leeds/Bradford | *From King's Cross* |
| 5.28 | York | *From Peterborough* |
| 5.34 | Hull | *From King's Cross* |
| 7.24 | Leeds/Bradford | *From Newark* |
| 7.32 | York | *From Newark* |
| 7.58 | Hull | *From Liverpool Central* |
| 8.22 | Leeds/Bradford/Harrogate | *The Yorkshire Pullman* |
| 8.28 | Hull | *The Yorkshire Pullman* |
| 9.5 | Leeds/Bradford | *From King's Cross* |
| 9.16 | Leeds/Bradford/Halifax | *From K. Cross* |
| 9.26 | Hull | *From King's Cross* |
| 10.5 | Hull | *From King's Cross* |
| 11.21 | Glasgow | *From Colchester* |
| 11.33 | Newcastle | *From King's Cross* |
| 11.52 | Edinburgh | *From King's Cross* |

**am**

| | | |
|---|---|---|
| 1.51 FX | King's Cross | *Sleeper from Newcastle & Sunderland* |
| 2.10 MX | K. Cross | *Sleeper from Edinburgh.* |
| 2.16 MO | King's Cross. | *From Darlington* |
| 2.28 FO | King's Cross | *Sleeper from Newcastle, Sunderland & Saltburn* |
| 4.1 | King's Cross | *Sleeper from Aberdeen & Elgin* |
| 4.8 MO | Lincoln Central | *From King's Cross* |
| 5.2 | Colchester via Peterborough | *From Glasgow* |
| 8.23 | King's Cross | *The West Riding* |
| 8.51 | King's Cross | *From Bradford/Leeds* |
| 9.52 MO | King's Cross | *13/7-24/8 From Darlington* |
| 10.6 | King's Cross | *From York* |
| 10.24 TThO | King's Cross | *From Sunderland* |
| 10.37 | Liverpool Central | *From Hull* |
| 11.12 MTFO | Yarmouth | *6/7 - 7/9  From York* |
| 11.12 MO | Lowestoft | *13/7 - 31/8 From Newcastle* |
| 11.42 | King's Cross | *The Yorkshire Pullman* |

**pm**

| | | |
|---|---|---|
| 12.35 FO | King's Cross | *From 26th June* |
| 12.52 | King's Cross. | *From Ripon, Leeds/Bradford* |
| 1.49 | King's Cross | *From Hull* |
| 2.25 FO | King's Cross | *From Bradford/Leeds* |
| 2.43 | King's Crsss | *From Bradford/Leeds* |
| 3.42 | Colchester | *From Newcastle* |
| 4.30 | King's Cross | *The White Rose* |
| 4.40 | King's Cross | |
| 5.30 FO | Liverpool Central | *From Hull* |
| 5.36 | Liverpool Central | *From Hull* |
| 6.30 | King's Cross | *From Hull* |
| 7.19 FX | King's Cross | *From Newcastle* |
| 7.24 FO | King's Cross | *FromLeeds/Bradford* |
| 7.43 | Swindon | *From Scarborough* |
| 11.15 | King's Cross | *From Newcastle* |
| 11.28 FO | Paignton | *From Hull* |
| 11.40 | Peterborough | *FromBradford/Leeds* |

On top of these were local trains to Hull at 12.25MO, 1.22MX, 6.0 and 9.0am, and at 4.0, 4.41, 5.8, 6.15(*Mon-Thurs & Fri 19/6*), and 6.27pmFO *From 26/6*; to Sheffield Victoria at 2.44, 5.15, 6.45, 7.45, 8.27 and 9.40am, and 12.25, 2.5, 3.40, 4.55, 6.28, 8.50 and 10.16pm; to Sheffield Midland at 10.25am; to Retford at 2.54am; to Newark at 6.50pm; to Leeds Central at 5.25, 7.28, 9.6, 11.15am, and 8.54 and 10.22pm; to Leeds and Bradford at 6.20am and 12.55, 2.58, 5.12 and 5.44pm; to Cleethorpes at 5.49 and 9.14am, and 12.16, 1.52, 2.52, 5.39 and 9.20pm; to March at 6am; to Peterborough via Lincoln, Sleaford and Spalding at 9.11am; to York at 7.32, 8.12, 8.52 and 11.7am, and 3.5, 8.12 and 10.15pm

Altogether there were approximately 120 departures from Doncaster every 24 hours with an average of one every 11 minutes between 6am and 6pm. On top of these were terminating trains arriving from Hull, Cleethorpes, Leeds and Bradford, Sheffield, York and Lincoln.

In 1981 the station was being used by 200 passenger trains a day  with 30 more passing through.

Above: A trainside newsvendor completes this early 1960s scene as B1 4-6-0 No. 61012 *Puku* is coupled to the Hull portion of the Yorkshire Pullman, left by the main train at the far south end of the station. *(N.E.Stead collection)*

Below: The protype Deltic was a big attraction during layovers between working the 8.50am from King's Cross and the 1.49pm return in 1959. But the 22 production models which followed in 1961 spelt the end for East Coast Main Line steam . *(BR photo/D. Porter collection)*

Bellcode's Stephen Chapman visited Doncaster only once in steam days but what he saw during a brief moment in August, 1959 was enough to hook him on railways for good.

"As our Colchester-Newcastle train pulled into the station I saw a big blue American-style diesel standing in one of the bay platforms. It had a large headlight on the bonnet and yellow cat's whisker stripes on the front. It was, of course, the prototype Deltic though I doubt if I recognised it at the time.

"What followed next I certainly did recognise. Backing through the station light engine was an absolutely immaculate, probably ex-works, *Mallard.*

"That pleasurable double vision through my carriage window all those years ago has stuck in my mind's photo album ever since."

Vintage class at Doncaster. Top: The GN J6 0-6-0s dating from 1911 were a development by H.A. Ivatt of his J5s, introduced in 1909. In 1950 nearly all the surviving J5s were allocated to Colwick shed. No. 65487 looked almost on its last legs when working a short pick-up goods at 5pm on 16th April, 1952.

Centre: When Gresley took over at the GNR he altogether preferred bigger engines and wasted no time in producing his first Pacifics. Fifty minutes before the J5 passed through, A3 No. 60044 *Melton*, still with single chimney and wearing either early BR blue or apple green, called at platform 4 with the Leeds to King's Cross White Rose.
*(Both David Holmes)*

Bottom: Ivatt introduced his large boilered 4-4-2 Atlantics in 1902 and they were prime East Coast power until Gresley's Pacifics came along in the 1920s, all being withdrawn by the start of the 1950s. It was early BR days and New England's 62839 was still wearing its LNER colours when preparing to leave platform one with a semi-fast to Grantham.
*(N.E.Stead collection)*

## SHORT MEMORIES

**26.4.60:** B12/3 4-6-0 No. 61572 and Midland Compound 4-4-0 No. 1000 double-head an Ian Allan excursion from King's Cross to Doncaster.

**August, 1960:** D11s 62662/4/7/9 and J15 0-6-0 65479 arrive for scrap.

**Summer holiday moguls.**
**Above:  The last working member of its class,  K2 No. 61760 was having a final fling with a return excursion from Bridlington when calling at platform 4 at 7.53pm on 1st August, 1960.**
*(David Holmes)*

**Below:  Some years  before the above picture and before the platforms were re-roofed, K3/2 No. 61822 was on a similar working.  The spotters pay only passing attention to it though - imagine the fuss if one turned up today.** *(Norman Ling / P. Rose collection)*

*In  1959 the second class single fare from Doncaster to King's Cross was 26 shillings(£1.30)*

# SHORT MEMORIES

**Summer, 1960:** Stored D49 4-4-0s returned to service to help overcome a motive power shortage are booked to work the 8.47am Hull-Doncaster and 1.44pm return, the 5.53pm Hull-Doncaster and the 8.26pm Yorkshire Pullman return on Mondays to Fridays. They have one return working on Saturdays.

**August, 1960:** The first two Doncaster-built 25kv electric locos for the West Coast Main Line are taking shape at the Plant.

**Above:** The driver of B1 No. 61365 watches for the guard's setting back signal before propelling the 9am from Grimsby back out of the station on 31st August, 1954. ( *Brian Morrision*)

**Below:** The railway reached all parts of Doncaster, even the streets. This small diesel locomotive was built by Ruston and Hornsby of Lincoln in 1960 and the British Road Services (Pickfords) low loader was delivering it to Rowntree's chocolate factory in York. (*Derek Porter*)

Above: Apart from the expresses and various other passenger trains, a continuous procession of goods and coal trains helped to fill the enthusiasts' notebooks with various classes of 2-8-0. Original ex-GC O4/1 No. 63576 was clanking along the Down Main with a Class 9 goods composed mainly of empty coal wagons on 7th May, 1963. *(David Holmes)*

Below: From the opposite end of the opposite platform with Doncaster North signal box to the left, WD 2-8-0 No. 90538 trundles a long train of 24.5 ton mineral wagons into the north end of platform 4 on 17th June, 1965. *(Peter Rose)*

Above: Another pair of foreigners reaching Doncaster with a railtour but Darlington works was the attraction for the Railway Correspondence and Travel Society's East Midlander from Nottingham Victoria on 13th May, 1962. SR Schools 4-4-0 No. 30925 *Cheltenham* and Midland 2P 4-4-0 No. 40646 approach the station with the return train. This special covered so much ground that it also features in Railway Memories Nos. 1, 2 and 6. *(Derek Porter)*

Below: In summers 1965 and 66 a Leeds Holbeck Jubilee 4-6-0 was often turned out for the 4.50pm Leeds to Doncaster stopping train and 6.3pm return. Holbeck engineman Roy Wood took this photo from 45675 *Hardy* while entering Doncaster station with the 4.50pm from Leeds on 19th August, 1965.

*The 1960 Eastern Region Sectional Appendix stated that diesel multiple units may haul one 4-wheel or 6-wheel van, provided the load does not exceed 17 tons, between Gainsborough and Doncaster, Sheffield and Doncaster, Doncaster and Cleethorpes, and Doncaster and Leeds Central.*

Top: On 17th June, 1965 B1 No. 61050 was marshalling its train of empty coaches alongside "C" box on the Goods lines through Doncaster West yard, between the station and the Plant. *(Peter Rose)*

Centre: In the mid-1960s a Derby Works DMU split the points and tried to go in two directions at once. It is seen next to South box shortly after its escapade. *(Derek Porter)*

Bottom: When the streets of many a town were every bit as fascinating as its railway. This trolley bus's pole had come off the wires near Hexthorpe Road bridge, as often happened there. *(Derek Porter)*

**Above: One of the L1 2-6-4Ts transferred to Doncaster in October, 1960, No. 67780 was deployed as a station pilot in the north end bay platforms at 12.20pm on 7th November, 1961.** *(David Holmes)*

**Below: Pressed into action as station pilot after leaving the works, King's Cross suburban N2 0-6-2T No. 69546 was stood with vans in the north end bay on 24th May, 1959.** *(Neville Stead)*

Owing to gaps in track circuiting, locomotives of 8' 6" wheelbase or less must not travel over main running lines without at least one vehicle attached...Locomotives with a wheelbase of 19ft or less shunting at Doncaster station must always have a fitted vehicle attached with the vacuum brake operating. The vehicle may be in front or rear of the pilot and will form part of the locomotive. *ER Sectional Appendix, 1960.*

Station pilots could be called to assist departing trains and the 1960 Sectional Appendix gave the following instruction: "In order to reduce the strain on engines in starting heavy loads, main line passenger trains may be assisted in the rear when starting from Doncaster station. The assisting engine must not be attached to the train, and will render assistance for approximately TWO COACH LENGTHS ONLY in order to provide initial impetus. The asistance should be provided for all heavy trains of 16 or more coaches where it can be done without inconvenience to traffic movements.

Two pilots were kept at the north end of the station. One always stood on the turntable facing the direction of the next anticipated job. This could include banking assistance on the avoiding line.

Above: A fascinating view of the north end of Doncaster station from North Bridge on 12th May, 1959. J6 0-6-0 No. 64259 shunts empty coaches with the fish dock on its left. The buildings along the background include the Salvation Army hall and John Line & Sons paint, wallpaper and varnish store. Gresley House towers over the 1930s station building but the ugly multi-storey car park was still just a twinkle in a developer's eye. *(Neville Stead)*

Below: The neat looking J52 0-6-0STs were introduced by Ivatt in 1897. No. 68849 trips empty wagons under North Bridge and towards the station on 31st August, 1954. *(Brian Morrison)*

**Above:** With trolley bus wires overhead, A3 No. 60112 *St. Simon* rolls under North Bridge with a Glasgow to King's Cross express on 31st August, 1954. The bridge was completed in 1910, replacing a congested level crossing. *(Brian Morrison)*

**Below:** Shortly after the express, J11 0-6-0 No. 64404 hauls a Through Freight under North Bridge on its way from the Grimsby line to the Sheffield area. Note the photographers peering over the parapet. *(Brian Morrison)*

**Above:** Another special, this time for the William Deacons Bank Club, crosses the River Don bridge just north of Marshgate Junction and heads for York behind Southern Region Merchant Navy Pacific No. 35026 *Lamport & Holt Line.* The Leeds lines are on the right while Marshgate goods yard and St. George's church are in the left background. *(N.E.Stead collection)*

**Below:** Work in 1909 on the River Don new cut being undertaken in association with construction of the North Bridge, complete with rail-mounted vertical boilered steam crane. *(D. Porter collection)*

*In 1957 the former G C Marshgate goods yard was shown as equipped to handle coal, mineral and wagonload traffic.*

*The yard consisted of seven sidings, two forming a loop, an outside platform goods shed, a crane and a siding serving a fertilizer depot.*

*Marshgate closed on 30th April, 1971 by which time it had been reduced to an unstaffed public delivery siding. The yard subsequently became a railway civil engineers' depot and remained so in 1997.*

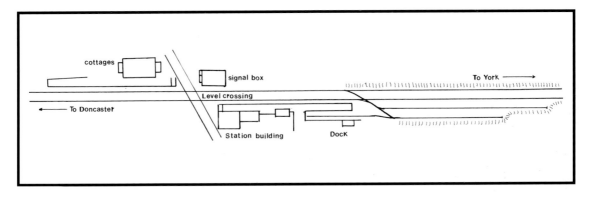

**Above: The layout at Arksey station in 1961**(*Not to scale*)

**Centre: Shaftholme Junction marks the northern limit of the Doncaster area.. Wakefield-based WD 2-8-0 No. 90054 follows the original GN line to Askern on 29th May, 1961. The furthest of the two overbridges carried the H&B and GC Joint line from Aire Jn. to Bullcroft Jn.**
*(Peter Rose)*

**Bottom: The modernistic Shaftholme Junction signal box, photographed as V2 2-6-2 No. 60858 heads past with a southbound express goods on the same day.**
*(Peter Rose)*

In summer, 1946 the LNER ran a scant stopping service between Doncaster and York. Down trains left Doncaster at 7.25am, 11.20am and 6.35pm, all calling at Arksey five minutes later. Up trains left York at 8.20am, calling Arksey at 9.19, and 4.50pm, calling Arksey at 5.52. Other local trains left Doncaster at 8.26am and York at 3.15pm and 6.5pm serving Selby but missing most smaller stations, including Arksey. The service was no better in 1997. The small stations were long closed and the only trains were the 05.52 and 20.46 Doncaster-Selby, the 06.16 Selby-Doncaster and 18.58 Hull-Sheffield via Selby and Doncaster.

Left: Two and a half miles before Doncaster St. James on the South Yorkshire Railway from Mexborough, the line passed the limestone quarry of Yorkshire Amalgamated Products Ltd. and its associated sidings at Warmsworth. In 1975 1958-built Ruston and Hornsby 4-wheel diesel *Charles* was the company's shunter there. *(Stephen Chapman)*

A station at Warmsworth lasted only until 1875. The GC ran Warmsworth Lime Siding until 1916 when it became a private siding.

# SOUTH YORKSHIRE'S OWN RAILWAY

Below: Before they reach Doncaster, trains from the Sheffield direction have to negotiate limestone hills through a sheer-sided rock cutting between Warmsworth and Hexthorpe where the landscape opens out again to reveal the Doncaster railway environment. During 1962, WD 2-8-0 No. 90153 passes Warmsworth lime sidings and signal box before plunging into the cutting with a Doncaster-bound coal train. The vertical cutting walls have been a constant headache for railway engineers battling to prevent rock falls. The picture shows a couple of spots where crumbling limestone has been patched with blocks. *(Derek Porter)*

Above: Just east of Warmsworth is Hexthorpe Junction where the Doncaster avoiding line to Bentley Junction diverges. On the same day as the WD opposite, Class 04/7 2-8-0 No. 63843 stands on the avoiding line waiting the road to its home depot at Mexborough. *(Derek Porter)*

Below: After the confines of Warmsworth cutting came the expanse of Hexthorpe 'Flats' sidings, occupied on a warm summer's day by Mexborough J11 No. 64377. *(Derek Porter)*

HEXTHORPE JN. - ST. JAMES JN. Working over Up and Down Goods lines on Sundays. Drivers of trains cautioned into the Up Goods line at Hexthorpe Jn. and into the Down Goods line at St. James Jn. on Sundays during the time Balby Bridge box is closed, must be prepared to stop short of trains standing at Balby Bridge taking water. *Eastern Region Sectional Appendix, 1960.*

St. James Bridge station was deadly quiet on this day but, being purely an excursion platform, it was a hive of activity on race days when many special trains arrived there instead of choking up the main station. Mexborough J11 No. 64403 was on either express passenger or pilot duty when caught alongside St. James Bridge in the 1950s. *(G. Oats)*

---

## THORNE - WARMSWORTH(VIA AVOIDING LINE) 1968

*Maximum speed on main lines* ....................60mph
*Maximum speed on goods lines*....................30mph

*Additional Lines*   Thorne(Kirton Lane)-Bentley Junction(Up and Down Goods)
Thorne Junction(Down Goods loop with standage for 93 wagons, engine and brake van).
Bentley Junction(Four Up refuge sidings. Two have standage for 20 wagons, engine and brake van, one with standage for 26 wagons, engine and brake, and one with standage for 32 wagons, engine and brake).

*Signalling*   Absolute Block on main lines.
Permissive Block on goods lines(Kirton Lane-Bentley Jn./ Bentley Jn.-Sprotborough-Hexthorpe Jn.

*Signal boxes*   Stainforth Jn.(1 mile 1088yds from Thorne Jn.); Barnby Dun Station(2 miles 257yds*); Kirk Sandall Jn.(1692yds*); Bentley Jn.(2 miles 520yds*); Sprotborough(2 miles 863yds*); Hexthorpe Jn.(1217yds*); Warmsworth(1409yds*) *Distance from previous box*

*Absolute Block signalling was in force on the avoiding line on summer Saturdays when passenger trains not stopping at Doncaster were routed that way.*

# SHORT MEMORIES

**13.8.60:** Brush Type 2 diesel D5525 replaces the usual V2 2-6-2 as far as York on the 7.15am Colchester-Newcastle. Sulzer Type D5060 works the 10.52am Doncaster-Yarmouth.

**Autumn 1960:** Ex-LMS Compound 4-4-0s 40907 and 41063 arrive at the Plant for scrapping.

**October, 1961:** Brush diesel prototype *Falcon* regularly works the 8.15am King's Cross-Hull as far as Doncaster while on trial. It also works overnight King's Cross-Edinburgh parcels trains to Doncaster and back

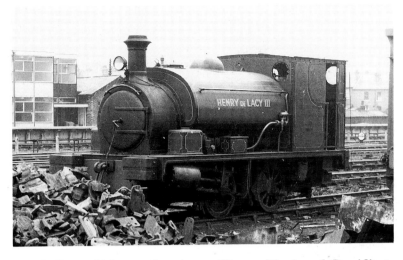

Above: Scrap dealers and engineers Thomas Ward used the sidings at Cherry Tree Lane where they received engines for scrapping. Hudswell Clarke 0-4-0ST *Henry de Lacy 111*, built in 1940,was awaiting its fate there on 31st March, 1968. (*Adrian Booth*)

Below: Quite a few people got carried away and put themselves in considerable danger when West Country Pacific No. 34094 *Mortehoe* arrived in Doncaster with the Warwickshire Railway Society special of 12th May, 1963. Scrap was piling up in Cherry Tree Lane goods yard and beyond that was the Doncaster cold store. (*N.E.Stead collection*)

From the late 1940s to the mid-1950s Harry Watling worked on a major River Don improvement scheme next to the railway at Marshgate.

"This involved widening, deepening and straightening the river from Crimpsall to Kirk Sandall and beyond. In 1953 we worked very close to Marshgate sidings which were only a few yards from the river. We were pile driving along the river bank, very close to the bridge carrying the line from Hull and Grimsby.

"A weight limit on this bridge meant the heaviest loco, and the main workhorse, on this line was the B1. Each morning just before 11.30 we saw the Hull section of the Yorkshire Pullman headed by a B1 cross the bridge to join the Leeds section at Doncaster station and form the 11.30 to King's Cross.

"All the steel piles we used came in by rail to Marshgate sidings.

"About a mile down river of the bridge we built a weir. The foundations used hundreds of tons of boiler clinker which also came via the sidings. We had to shovel it out of railway wagons into barrows, wheel it over wooden staging and tip it into the river.

"The purpose of the weir was to keep a constant depth of water around the railway bridge and control the flow of water around the bridge supports to prevent them being washed away.

"Marshgate sidings was a haven for railway enthusiasts. On Friday afternoons we were sometimes teated to the gem of the collection. The A4 look-alike 4-6-4 No. 60700 would be in the sidings being made ready for a late afternoon run to points north or south of Doncaster. The driver was often a neighbour of mine, Arthur Renney, a lifelong railwayman.

" We saw Beyer Garratts on the avoiding line."

**Below: Harry Watling took this photo while working on the River Don scheme in 1953. B1 No. 61304 has just got the road from the signal and is rolling on to the restricted bridge with the Hull portion of the Yorkshire Pullman to King's Cross. The avoiding line is on the distant embankment.**

*On Mondays-Fridays in winter 1956/57 24 Up and 26 Down booked passenger class trains used the Doncaster-Stainforth line. There were four Hull-King's Cross expresses each way, plus a 10.30am from London as required and an 8.43pm from Grantham. Others were the 9.24am and 4.13pm Hull-Liverpool Central and 9.30am and 4.30pm from Liverpool, three Doncaster to Hull and two return, two Hull to Sheffield Victoria, one return, plus one Hull-Sheffield Midland each way, the Up train an express, the Down a stopper. There were also three Doncaster to Hull stoppers(two starting at Sheffield Victoria) and six from Hull. A Doncaster-Dairycoates empty stock train was booked each way plus an extra from Dairycoats as required. On the Grimsby line were seven Down and six Up Doncaster-Cleethorpes stoppers(one through to Penistone and one Down train from Gainsborough Central). The only express was the 1.5am Mondays Only Manchester London Road-Cleethorpes news.*

**Mexborough WD 2-8-0 No. 90580 comes off the avoiding line at Bentley Junction with an eastbound mixed goods in 1963.** *(D. Collingwood)*

EAST MIDLANDS GAS BOARD SIDINGS - COLD STORE SIDINGS - BOWSER, MONKS & WHITEHOUSE SIDINGS - S. PARKINSON & SON(DONCASTER) LTD. SIDINGS - INTERNATIONAL HARVESTER CO. LTD SIDINGS - WHEATLEY PARK GOODS DEPOT. Access to these sidings is by means of a trunk line extending from Marshgate goods sidings(and also a connection from the Down Main line west of Marshgate Goods Siding box)to Wheatley Park with loop sidings west of the river bridge and level crossing at Milethorpe Lane, at the entrance to Messrs. Radiance Ltd. works, at International Harvester Company's works, and also the occupation crossing from Borrill Avenue to Wheatley Hall farm.

An engine or vehicles must not be taken past the converging point of the loop nearest to Marshgate goods siding until the permission of the shunter or other person in charge has been obtained. A stop board is provided at this point.

When vehicles are placed in the Loop lines the engine must not be detached until the vehicles have been properly secured by means of hand brakes, and when an engine is attached to vehicles standing in either of the Loop lines for the purpose of removing them, any other vehicles left in the same siding must be properly secured.

With the exception of the level crossing gates from Borrill Avenue to Wheatley Hall farm, which are kept locked against the road when not in use, the gates of the level crossings must be kept locked across the railway except when it is necessary to open them for a trip to pass in either direction. Trips must be stopped before reaching each crossing to enable the man in charge of the trip to unlock and open the gates, after satisfying himself that all is in order for this to be done, and must again be stopped after clearing the crossing for the main in charge to relock the gates across the line. It is essential the gates should not be left across the road longer than is necessary for the passing of each trip. *Eastern Region Sectional Appendix, 1960.*

*The goods depot set up by the LNER to serve Wheatley Park industrial estate was equipped to handle coal, mineral and wagon load traffic. Classed as a public delivery siding, it closed in August, 1971 with the rest of this railway.*

*Auxiliary token instruments were provided in huts next to the Down Branch(SYJ) second home and Up Branch starting signals at Kirk Sandall Jn. If a train was held at the Down Branch second home , drivers were instructed to put the token in the appropriate auxilliary instrument. If stood at the Up Branch starting signal, they had to, unless the indicator on the token instrument showed 'free', telephone the Kirk Sandall signalman and act on his instructions.If the indicator showed 'free' the token was extracted according to instructions on the instrument*

In 1955, at the age of 15, David Bell gave up the fresh air of the countryside for a job in the cellars beneath Doncaster station.

With another 15 year-old, it was his job to bring in the supplies of beer and soft drinks for the buffet and to clear out the empties and rubbish.

"We took dustbins to a wagon in the dock at the north end of the station, near where the multi-storey car park is now. We emptied out the rubbish every morning and brought new supplies in.

"Stock came by lorry to the parcels office where we collected it. We had to push a platform barrow piled high with crates of beer and soft drinks. Getting safely past all the people on the station was tricky. We used a lift to reach the platforms.

"What wasn't sold during the day went to the little night buffet on platform 4, at the top of the subway stairs. The two day buffets closed at 10pm which was when the night buffet opened, but it only sold tea and cakes.

"From 16 I was a junior number taker at Pilkington's sidings, Kirk Sandall, logging all the wagons in and out, and putting labels on them.

"Wagons went all over the country, a lot to various docks. They had 'tower' wagons designed to carry three big sheets of glass, well wagons and smaller wagons. Across the way, sand came to the Rockware factory and still does."

In 1958 he moved on to Barnby Dun station as an 18 year old porter.

"The station was quiet but I had to be at work by 5.45am for the first train which brought the Pilkington's workers. I worked until 1.30 or 2pm.

"My job included putting up posters and changing signal lamps which meant walking miles along the line. We had 10 lamps or more kept ready as replacements for emergencies. We took two freshly filled and trimmed lamps out and brought back two we replaced. We did that every Tuesday and Wednesday, whatever the weather.

"There wasn't much parcels traffic, just railway mail. A few wagons came into the sidings bringing sacks for farmers who sent out peas and potatoes. There was little maltings traffic by then.

"You could always look down the line and see a goods train. Traffic was mostly coal, steel and fish. We reckoned that if a train had 50 wagons it was empty and loaded if it had 36 on. I loved to see the Beyer-Garratts go through pulling 120 wagons.

"In 1961 I returned to Pilkington's but then came Beeching, our staff was cut from three to one and I left the railway."

**Below: Barnby Dun station and signal box looking towards Doncaster in early 1967. Despite the rundown look of the buildings and closure just a few months away, the platform garden remains well kept.** *(Peter Rose)*

**In winter 1956/7 Barnby Dun had trains to Doncaster at 7.50, 8.50 and 9.26am, 2.38, 4.55, 8.5 and 8.26pm, to Sheffield Victoria at 7.29am, to Cleethorpes at 5.58 and 9.22am, 3.1, 5.37 and 9.10pm, to Hull at 10.58am and 4.8, 5.11 and 6.30pm, and the 4.55pm Hull-King's Cross called there at 5.51.**

**The station and goods yard could handle goods, parcels and miscellaneous traffic, livestock, horse boxes and prize cattle vans while a siding served G. F. Milnthorp Ltd.'s maltings. Goods facilities were withdrawn on 5th April, 1965 and the passenger station closed on 4th September, 1967, but the buildings were still there 30 years later.**

**Stainforth and Hatfield had extensive sidings for staging and sorting coal traffic generated by local pits until the 1980s rundown of the mining industry. Class O2/2 2-8-0 No. 63936 was handling such traffic in the Down sidings at 2.52pm on 7th May, 1963 while wagons lined the top of the bank at Hatfield Colliery.** *(David Holmes)*

Mrs. Cynthia Finch joined the recently nationalised railway in October, 1948 and was sent to work as a clerk at Stainforth & Hatfield.

"The station had Up and Down platforms and a signal box which was manned 24 hours a day. There were two offices. One was for passenger tickets, booking parcels, receiving time sheets, goods guards' work sheets(journals) and the like. I worked in this one along with two male clerks and the station master. We had a cast iron stove which we fed with coal and high chairs up to a sloping desk. There was a huge staff at Stainforth and we were very busy.

"Besides two clerks in the now demolished goods office, we had inspectors round the clock in the goods yard, along with passenger and goods guards, shunters, porters and lampmen.

"The time sheets from all the staff were worked out for normal hours, extra to an eight hour day at time and a half and Sunday at double time. Minimum pay was in operation.

"I would have to help the other clerks to put cash in each envelope that I had written the man's name on. A hand-worked machine was used for sending messages to other stations on a code. It clicked and clicked.

"You saw few cars parked at the station in those days as most of us travelled to work at Stainforth by train or bicycle."

About 1953, Mrs. Finch moved away to Thorne North and five years later to Thorne South.

"This small station dealt with steel fromScunthorpe for Richerd Dunston's shipbuilding firm, keeping one Scammel lorry driver busy most of the time. We also received piles of parcels for delivery to local shops by a second driver. Money collected for tickets and luggage was sent by train to Doncaster booking office in a leather bag.

*ENGINES TAKING WATER AT DOWN BRANCH LINE WATER COLUMNS. A telephone is provided at the Down Branch line water columns and on completion of taking water drivers must advise the signalman at Stainforth Junction box that the train is ready to proceed.( ER Sectional Appendix)*

**Above: Class O1 2-8-0 No. 63646 from Staveley shed trundles past stainforth and Hatfield station and its Down sidings with a class 8 train of empty bogie bolster wagons for Scunthorpe on 7th May, 1963. The O1s were O4s modernised from 1944 onwards with standard 100A boilers, Walschaerts valve gear and new cylinders.**

**Below: On the same day, No. 63936 makes a smokey departure from the Up sidings while returning west with a  class 9 goods.** *(Both David Holmes)*

In winter 1956/57, Stainforth & Hatfield was served by 19 Down and 16 Up passenger trains a day on Mondays to Fridays. They left for Hull at 5.50, 6.15, 9.13 and 11.5am, 12.46, 4.15, 5.17, 6.37 and 8.14pm; for Cleethorpes at 6.6 and 9.30am, 12.30, 1.46, 3.8, 5.23, 5.44 and 9.18pm, for Doncaster at 7.45, 8.45, 9.21, 9.46 and 11.51am, 2.33, 8.0, 8.21 and 9.51pm, for Sheffield Victoria at 7.24am, Liverpool Central at 10.51am(WFX) and 5.14pm, for Penistone at 4.50pm, and for King's Cross at 5.46pm. The 4.30am from Hull terminated there at 5.33, while two trains from Doncaster called there at 12.38am and 3.38am when required for Stainforth trainmen only.

By comparison, the winter 1996/7 service from the station, renamed Hatfield & Stainforth, stands at three trains to Hull, 14 to Scunthorpe, 14 to Goole, six to Sheffield and 25 to Doncaster.

**April, 1962:** AC electric locos E3073-7/87/88 under construction at the Plant.

**11.9.62**: A3 No. 60042 *Singapore* works the 5.30am Doncaster-Sheffield Vic. parcels.

**April, 1963**: The 6.26pm King's Cross-Doncaster is steam-hauled again.

**25.5.63:** Steam locos noted on Carr Loco include Britannia 70009 *Alfred the Great(31B)*, A1s 60128 *Bongrace*, 60158 *Aberdonian*, and a selection of WD 2-8-0s, 9F 2-10-0s and B1 4-6-0s. Under repair at the Plant were three Deltics, A3 60063 *Isinglass* and WDs 90043/88/602/719, and ex-works A1 60152 *Holyrood*(64B).

**May, 1963:** The summer timetable leaves just one daily Leeds-King's Cross steam diagram - the 4am from King's Cross and the Up White Rose.

**Summer, 1963:** Diesel prototype DP2 spends six weeks passing through Doncaster with the 10.10am King's Cross-Edinburgh and 10.30pm return.

**Sept.1963**: Diesel prototype No. D0260 *Lion* starts working the 4am King's Cross-Leeds and the southbound Yorkshire Pullman.

On heath land near Hatfield is a little known but extensive railway. The 3ft gauge network, used by the horticulture division of Fisons Plc for collecting peat from the moss lands, was still operating in 1996, owing its survival to the fact that the boggy ground cannot support heavy road vehicles. The lightweight track can also be easily repositioned as turf cutting progresses.
As illustrated above, quite long trains run between the moss and the works where wagons are discharged by tippler(below).
In April, 1977 when these pictures were taken, Fisons had a fleet of six diesel mechanical locomotives consisting of one 1964-built Lister Blackstone, two Motor Rail Simplex's, one built in 1967 and one in 1971, two Hunslets built in 1974 and one German Diema, also built in 1974. One of the Simplex's is shown above hauling a long trainload of peat from the moss to the works.
By 1994 the fleet still stood at six including three modern locomotives - one a powerful master and slave unit - built in 1990 by German company Schoma.
*(Both Stephen Chapman)*

Above: A gleaming B1, No. 61017 *Bushbuck* and equally immaculate train of empty stock rolls effortlessly down the West Riding & Grimsby Doncaster leg towards Marshgate Junction in the early 1960s. The engine and stock look as though they could be ex-works and returning from a test run as they pass under the Doncaster avoiding line. *(D. Collingwood)*

# THE WEST RIDING AND GRIMSBY

Below: Further out along the West Riding & Grimsby, K1 2-6-0 No. 62055 attacks the 1 in 350 rise towards Doncaster while near Bentley with a class 8 goods. *(Derek Porter)*

Signalling on the West Riding & Grimsby main lines in 1968 was Absolute Block with Track Circuit Block on the Down Main between Doncaster and Castle Hills. Goods lines were Permissive Block. An Up Goods ran from Nostell to Hemwsorth and a Down Goods from Hemsworth South to Station.

Maximum speed on main lines was 70mph, 30mph on the Adwick-Stainforth line and 40mph on Goods lines.

Signal boxes were at Bentley Crossing, Castle Hills, Carcroft Station, Adwick Junction, Moorhouse Junction, South Kirkby Junction, Hemsworth South, Hemsworth Station and Fitzwilliam. The two intermediate boxes on the Stainforth-Adwick section were Applehurst Junction and Bramwith.

Gradients are gentle on this section but there is a steady climb from Carcroft to Fitzwilliam with two stretches of over a mile at 1 in 150 each.

**Right:** Until the early 1990s a branch ran to Brodsworth Colliery from the Doncaster-Wakefield line at Castle Hills Junction.
Here, Class 04/8 2-8-0 No. 63858 struggles to drag its heavy load from Brodsworth on to the main line in January, 1963. *(D. Collingwood)*

**Below:** Carcroft & Adwick Le Street station as it was in the early 20th century with a Leeds to King's Cross express being hauled through by what appears to be a GNR Ivatt. 4-2-2 Single.
This station closed in 1967 but a new one opened behind the photographer's vantage point in 1993. *(Lens of Sutton)*

**Above: Deltic No. 55014 *The Duke of Wellington's Regiment* comes off the spur from Carcroft Junction to join the Adwick - Stainforth line at Skellow Junction and the site of Bullcroft Colliery during diverions for the remodelling of Marshgate Junction in Spring 1979. A Brush Class 47 waits the road on the singled line from Adwick Junction with empty oil tanks returning to Immingham.** *(Neville Stead)*

**Below: Original GC O4/1 2-8-0 No. 63618 is pictured at Bramwith level crossing in the early 1960s with a short goods from Stainforth.** *(Derek Porter)*

The following passenger trains ran over the Stainforth-Adwick line on summer Saturdays in 1957: 8.14am Bradford-Cleethorpes; 8.47am and 4.13pm Leeds Central-Cleethorpes; 8.54am and 1.36pm Cleethorpes-Bradford, 9.5am Cleethorpes-Leeds, and 1.46pm Cleethorpes - Leeds and Bradford.

**Above: A3 Pacific No. 60082** *Neil Gow* **was running-in after overhaul at the Plant when it passed under the Hull and Barnsley Railway Denaby branch at Hampole with a Leeds to Doncaster stopping train on 30th August, 1961.** *(Peter Cookson)*

**Below: Moorhouse sidings formed a connection between the West Riding & Grimsby and the Hull and Barnsley's Wath branch giving access to Frickley and Hickleton collieries.**
**A3 No. 60063** *Isinglass* **passes by with a King's Cross to Leeds express on 23rd April, 1962.**
*(Peter Cookson)*

BULLCROFT COLLIERY. An electric gong for the guidance of drivers working trains of empty wagons to Bullcroft Colliery sidings, is fixed on a post 100 yards north of the inlet points to the arrival siding...a ringing key is provided on the north west corner of the weigh house. Guards must sound one long ring on this gong when they are ready for their train to set back into the sidings.
Drivers must not, after running round their trains, propel the wagons into the sidings until the guard has signalled on the gong that they may do so. After a locomotive has gone to the empties sidings... no further movement towards those sidings must be made within the Outer signals. *ER Sectional Appendix, 1960.*

**Above: South Elmsall, looking towards Doncaster, in late Victorian times.** *(Lens of Sutton)*

In steam days South Elmsall was a fairly quiet local station but what a thrill it must have been when the peace was shattered by the passage of an express like the Queen of Scots or the White Rose. On Mondays to Fridays in summer, 1957 it was served by 12 trains to Leeds, 10 to Doncaster and one direct to Cleethorpes. Most morning trains were to Leeds and most evening ones to Doncaster, catering for people working in Wakefield and Leeds. Families escaping for their annual holiday made for one of the Saturday Only excursions like the 7.45am to Skegness or the 9.51 to Cleethorpes.

South Elmsall enjoys the distinction of being the only small Doncaster-Leeds line station not to have closed at some stage but its staff and buildings have gone. In 1997 it was served by hourly Class 321 Leeds-Doncaster electric trains.

**Below: A1 No. 60115** *Meg Merriles* **rolls past the goods depot and into the station with a Doncaster-Leeds local in 1960. Goods facilities, which included a 10 ton yard crane, were closed in 1965.** *(Peter Cookson)*

## SHORT MEMORIES

**December, 1964:** The V2s enjoy a swansong deputising for diesels on freights to March.

**6.2.65:** Doncaster A1s 60128 and 60157 withdrawn.

**April, 1965:** 1000-ton block oil trains start using the Stainforth-Adwick line on their way between Immingham and a new terminal in Leeds.

**3.4.65:** B1s 61039/51/93 transferred to Doncaster from Canklow.

**19.6.65:** B1s 61050/5/8/1107/27/1208/1348/84; O4s 63688/734/8/85; WDs 90158/69/718 all move to Doncaster upon the closure of Retford shed.

Above: After South Elmsall, going towards Leeds, came the intersection with the Swinton & Knottingley line linking York and Sheffield; then came South Kirkby Junction where a line goes up to join the S&K at Moorthorpe, and then South Kirkby Colliery. Here, Ardsley B1 No. 61189 *Sir William Gray* passes the colliery and is about to pass under the S&K with a southbound express on 17th April, 1960. *(Peter Cookson)*

Below: Hunslet 0-6-0ST No. 9 *Kinsley,* built in Leeds in 1939, was still working at South Kirkby Colliery on 22nd September, 1972 when it was to be seen outside the loco shed. *(David Holmes)*

From Hemsworth Junction ran a west-east connection to the Hull and Barnsley main line which passed over the top.
Above: Class O2/1 2-8-0 No. 63922 plods along the Down Slow line towards Hemsworth with a class K goods, possibly the 2.50pm Doncaster Belmont to Ardsley, in September, 1960. *(Peter Cookson)*

Below: Looking west towards Hemsworth Junction from the H&B line, WD 2-8-0 No. 90342 heads along the Leeds-Doncaster line with a trainload of track panels on 4th June, 1962. The connections and sidings up to the H&B are on the right. *(Peter Rose)*

Above: Another one of Leeds Copley Hill's A1 Pacifics, No. 60117 *Bois Roussel* bowls along near Hemsworth with the Leeds Central to King's Cross White Rose on 21st June, 1960.

Below: Doncaster B1 4-6-0 No. 61087 leaves Fitzwilliam behind and runs in the direction of Nostell with a class E goods, probably the 6.30pm Doncaster Belmont to Ardsley Spring Lane, in the evening of 28th May, 1960. *(Both Peter Cookson)*

**Top:** After York Road ceased handling general freight in February, 1965, the site continued to be used by scrap dealers C.F. Booth until the rail connections were abandoned in late 1979.

A number of locomotives met their end there but Booth's regular shunter was Hudswell Clarke diesel No. D965, pictured on 24th March, 1976. *(Adrian Booth)*

**Centre:** Doncaster J39/2 0-6-0 No. 64885 has completed the morning shunt at York Road and is crossing the arches over marshland on its way out of the the station in June, 1960.
*(D. Collingwood)*

**Below:** York Road in the 1930s *(Not to scale)*

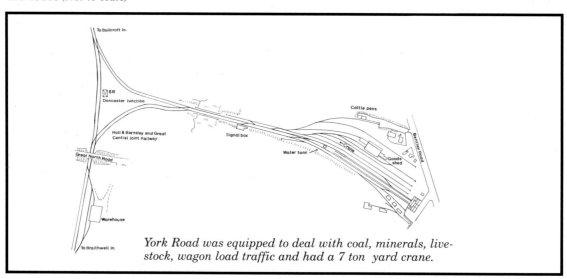

*York Road was equipped to deal with coal, minerals, livestock, wagon load traffic and had a 7 ton yard crane.*

# Doncaster private sidings, 1957

*The 1957 British Transport Commission Handbook of Stations listed 20 private sidings in Doncaster, collieries not included. Shown with main line access points, they were:*

Allan & Orr(GC line)
Arnold & Son(Belmont)
Arnold W. S.(GC line)
Bells wagon works, Red Bank
Briggs Motor Bodies Ltd.
British Ropes Ltd.(Belmont)
Thos. Burnett & Co. wagon works(GC line)
Darlington Fencing Co. Ltd. (Belmont)
Doncaster Co-op coal depot(Marshgate)
Doncaster Co-op coal depot(York Road)
Doncaster Highways Dept.(WR&G,Marshgate)

Doncaster Ice & Cold Store Co. (GC line)
Doncaster Wagon Co. (GC line)
East Midlands Gas Board(Marshgate)
International Harvester Co.(Wheatley Park)
Min. of Agriculture & Fisheries Food Store (Wheatley Park)
National Cold Stores(Management)Ltd. (Wheatley Park)
S. Parkinson & Sons Ltd.(Wheatley Park)
S.E.Stevens Ltd.(GC line)
Wagon Repairs Ltd. (GC line)

*In the 1960s the South Yorkshire Joint line was signalled by Absolute Block with Electric Token on the single lines (Maltby Colliery Sidings South to St. Catherine's and Low Ellers to Kirk Sandall.) It was double track from St. Catherine's to Low Ellers and down the 1,320-yard curve to Potterick Carr. Maximum speed was 25mph and the distance fromSt. Catherine's to Kirk Sandall 5.5 miles.*

*In the Doncaster area were signal boxes at St. Catherine's Jn, Low Ellers Jn, Markham Sidings and Kirk Sandall Jn. Markham box had no track circuiting and the view was obscured by trees and line curvature, so a 'treadle annunciator' was fitted to the track on the northern approach. This device warned the signalman of approaching trains by ringing a bell in the box when a train passed over it.*

**About a mile south of Kirk Sandall Junction , the SYJ served Markham Main Colliery.  Hunslet 0-4-0 diesel No. 7405 was shunting the colliery yard on 24th March, 1976.** *(Adrian Booth)*

MARKHAM SIDINGS. An auxiliary key token instrument has been fixed in a hut adjacent to Markham Sidings Down starting signal, and a telephone provided between the hut and Markham Sidings box.

In connection with key token working, drivers of Down trains will receive a token from the signalman at Markham Sidings box, and it will only be necessary to obtain a token from the auxiliary instrument when detained at the Down starting signal. Trains departing from the sidings in the Kirk Sandall direction must obtain a token from the auxiliary instrument. *Eastern Region Sectional Appendix, 1968.*

Like many collieries, Yorkshire Main had a narrow gauge railway for moving materials between the stock yard and the pit head, Hunslet diesel No. 3427, built 1946, was on the 3ft. gauge there in May, 1977.
*(Adrian Booth)*

*In 1968 the 3 mile 920-yard stump of the Dearne Valley Railway from Bessacarr Jn. to Yorkshire Main Sidings was signalled by Absolute Block with electric token between Black Carr Sidings West and Yorkshire Main Sidings.*

*It was a goods line and passenger trains were only allowed to use it on the authority of the movements manager.*

*Signal boxes were at Bessacarr Jn., Black Carr Sidings East, Black carr Sidings West, and Yorkshire Main Sidings.*

*Maximum line speed was 30mph.*

Authority to proceed from Yorkshire Main Sidings box to the colliery empty wagon sidings over the colliery running line will be given by the NCB staff man. He will hand the driver a token(Annett's key)and accompany the train to the empty wagon sidings and return with it to a point clear of the connections controlled from the NCB ground frame when the token must be returned to him.

Drivers returning from the empty wagon sidings to the loaded wagon sidings must not proceed past the stop board......until authorised to do so by the BR shunter. *Eastern Region Sectional Appendix, 1968.*

**On the standard gauge at Yorkshire Main Colliery, Leeds-built Hudswell Clarke 0-6-0ST No. 1178 was out of use on 22nd August, 1970.** *(Adrian Booth)*

*In 1964 Eastern Region management was reorganised into 5 divisions, one centred on Doncaster. First divisional manager was F. M. Wright, former GN line commercial superintendant, and Doncaster traffic manager since 1963.*

Above: Askern was the point where the first Great Northern line through Doncaster met the Lancashire and Yorkshire Railway and this was how the station looked in 1961, 14 years after its last timetabled passenger trains.

In 1957 the station and goods yard, which was equipped with a 5 ton crane, were shown as being able to handle a wide variety of goods, including motor cars, livestock, coal and parcels but it all came to an end when goods facilities were axed on 5th October, 1964. (*Peter Cookson*)

Below: Also at Askern were a colliery and the Doncaster Coalite company's coking plant. The colliery was home to a couple of NCB steam locomotives into the 1970s. One was Hunslet 0-6-0ST *Rossington No. 2*, pictured outside the engine shed on 12th september, 1972. (*David Holmes*)

*ROSSINGTON COLLIERY BRANCH. A cross-bar type semaphore signal is fixed where the NCB line crosses the Rossington branch near the colliery end of the loaded sidings. This signal will be operated by NCB staff, who will protect movements...to and from the empties sidings. The danger position of the signal is at right angles to the branch and the exhibition of a red light at night.*

SOUTH YORKS JOINT TO ROSSINGTON COLLIERY VIA ST. CATHERINE'S JN. In clear weather only, trains from the Tickhill direction to Rossington Colliery, if not more than 40 wagons, must run direct from St. Catherine's Jn. to Black Carr Sidings West, and then propel from there to Rossington Colliery...Drivers of trains requiring to travel via Black Carr Sidings West box..must whistle accordingly when passing Tickhill station. *Both from ER Sectional Appendix, 1960.*

# THE PLANT

Like any big railway works, Doncaster was an enthusiasts paradise, packed with rows of engines being built, overhauled or scrapped.

It gave generations of Doncaster citizens their livelihoods and a chance to leave their mark on the world. Together the Plant and Carr wagon works once employed 6,000 people.

Starting at just 11 acres the works grew eightfold producing locomotives, carriages and wagons for an expanding GNR. From 1890 to 1902 were added the new erecting shop, machine shop, the Crimpsall, tender and paint shops - and it continued evolving to meet the railway's changing needs.

In the 1960s, carriage building and overhauls ceased but loco work increased. The west and north carriage shops were converted for repairing diesel and building electric multiple units, and the main carriage shops to a wagon works replacing the Carr. A new diesel locomotive test house was built.

In 1968 the works came under BritishRail Engineering Ltd., allowing it to bid for external work including earth movers and hay bailers.

The new trains of the 1980s needed less maintenance so BR reviewed its workshop facilities. The Plant left BREL and was split into three. In 1987 the Crimpsall area became a 'major depot'

Some of the Plant's most distinguished creations arranged outside the paint shop ready for an open day on 17th June, 1978. From front to back, they are Patrick Stirling's 4-2-2 No.1, Ivatt's small boilered Atlantic *Henry Oakley* and large boilered 251, and two Gresley masterpieces - V2 2-6-2 *Green Arrow* and world speed record holding A4 *Mallard*. *(Derek Porter)*

where locos and multiple units would be overhauled in days rather than weeks by exchanging major components. The west and north DMU shops were converted into a national spare parts centre. The wagon shops, erecting shop and 1853 buildings became Doncaster Wagon Works and were sold as a going concern.

Doncaster built 2,223 locomotives and is believed to have done over 40,000 overhauls. Besides Gresley's famous Pacifics, notable engines include Patrick Stirling's No.1 of 1870 with its single pair of 8ft diameter driving wheels, Henry Ivatt's Atlantics for increasingly heavy trains, and in 1934 the revolutionary P2 2-8-2s, plus many goods and mixed traffic locos., the first bogie passenger coaches, Gresley's prolific teak bodied coaches, the 1930s streamlined sets and many all-steel BR Mk1s. It also built 42 BR Standard 4-6-0s, 70 2-6-0s and 10 2-6-4Ts. The first diesels built there were 0-6-0 shunters 15000-3 in 1944. Between 1957 and 87 came 24 DC electric locos, 80 AC locos including today's Class 86s, 112 diesel shunters and 135 Class 56 and 58 diesel locos.

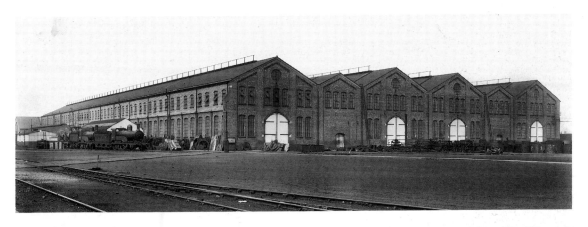

Above: The Crimpsall heavy repair shop was built between 1898 and 1900. Covering 140,000 sq ft of floor space it was the biggest of all the Plant shops and could always be relied upon to hold an awesome array of locomotives. This was the Crimpsall in June, 1923 with a pair of GNR 2-4-0s, including No. 867, waiting outside. *(Official photograph/Derek Porter collection)*

Below: A well-stocked Crimpsall shunter bay in 1966 with York's D3874 nearest on the right and three assorted Type 1s on the left. Nearest is one of the ill-fated North British locos in the D8400 series, the next an equally ill-starred British Thompson Houston of the D8200s while, furthest away alongside the Class 37 could be one of the more successful English Electric Class 20s. Thirty years later the Crimpsall workload had plummeted and it was facing a very doubtful future. *(BR photo/Derek Porter collection)*

**Above: The main Crimpsall erecting shop in 1966 with standard Eastern Region Brush Type 2 and English Electric Type 3 diesel locos under repair and, at the far end, a Deltic.**
*(BR Photo/Derek Porter collection)*

From 1960 the Plant overhauled BR Standard Class 5 4-6-0s from the Western Region. Some, like 73023 and 73068, were turned out in green livery

**Below: The layout at Doncaster Plant in March, 1972.** *(Not to scale)*

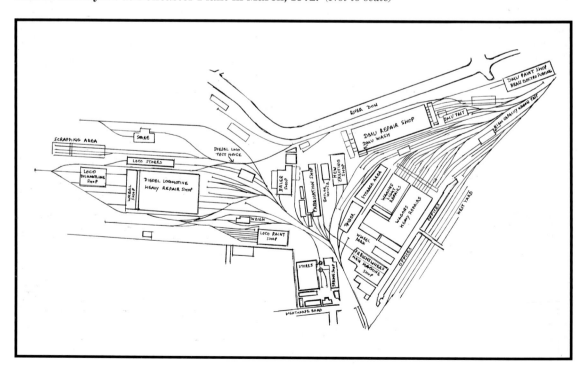

Above: In the 1960s the carriage shops were given over mainly to dealing with multiple units. Here, during 1966, Birmingham Railway Carriage & Wagon Co.-built(Class 104) motor composite No. NE50553 sits on the traverser which ran along the south end of the DMU shop. On the far right is the shed where units were washed before being overhauled.

Below: Inside the DMU shop in 1966 with various green-liveried vehicles present.
( *Both BR photos/Derek Porter collection*)

BR photos showing the wagon shops in 1966, shortly after modernisation and conversion from carriage shops.
Above: Looking north along the heavy repair shop. The building dates from 1948 as the original was devastated by fire in 1940.

Right: A wagon enters the light repair shop on the traverser.

**On 8th November, 1960, Peter Rose logged the following locomotives at the Plant:** Ivatt Class 4 2-6-0: 43094 from King's Lynn; 2P 4-4-0: 40491(55A)630(55E)90(55A); Compound 4-4-0 41157; Fowler 2-6-4T: 42365(9E)90(87E)9(9A); 3F 0-6-0: 43361; 2F 0-6-0: 58144; A4 4-6-2: 60010 *Dominion of Canada*(34A) 60018 *Sparrow Hawk*(52A); A3 4-6-2: 60055 *Woolwinder*(34A)60076 *Galopin*(52A)60077 *The White Knight*(52B)/60078 *Night Hawk*(52A)60106 *Flying Fox*(34F); A2/1 4-6-2 60510 *Robert the Bruce*(64A); B1 4-6-0: 61079/104/209/99/328/60/90; K3 2-6-0: 61859 (40B) 62 (31B)970(32A)5(56B); K1 2-6-0: 62068(31B); O2 2-8-0: 63959(36E); O4 2-8-0: 63915; J6 0-6-0: 64206/51(34E); J52 0-6-0ST: 68875(56B); J50 0-6-0T:68897(56B)901/43(56F)64(36A)71/91(34B); N2 0-6-2T: 69560(34F); Britannia 4-6-2: 70034 *Thomas Hardy*(32A); 4MT 2-6-0: 76024(52G); English Electric Type 4: D302/8; Barclay 0-6-0 diesel: D2403(40B); 350hp 0-6-0: D3475(40B).

Above: A beautifully panoramic view of the north end of the works yard taken from one of the lighting towers. The wagon shops are just off the picture to the right, the DMU shop on the left, and the North DMU paint shop and component store in the middle background with North Bridge crossing over the East Coast Main Line immediately behind it. *(BR Photo/D. Porter collection)*

Below: Looking the opposite way from North Bridge with a Brush Class 31 shunting DMU stock in the early 1980s. The wagon shops dominate the centre. *(Derek Porter)*

Above and opposite page top: Two splendid views of the works plate yard from the power house roof, next to the paint shop, on 29th March, 1946.

In the above picture, the Crimpsall shop is off to the left, then visible from the left are the timber drying shed, the fabrication and spring shops in front of the chimney, the next building contains the grinding, white metal and machine fitters shops, and the triple-roofed building on the right is the main machine shop. The opposite picture shows the iron foundry(two buildings left) and the boiler shop(three buildings right).

Below: The carriage drawing office in 1961.
*(Both official photos/Derek Porter collection)*

**Above: Situated behind the Crimpsall, the stripping shop was where loco-motives for classified repair were dismantled and the parts washed, cleaned and examined before going to the various repair sections.**
**On 3rd May, 1981 a stray spark from cutting equipment used by work-men stripping an oil tank caused this fire which was being attended by the local brigade.** *(Derek Porter)*

A British Transport Commission railway modernisation progress report stated that in 1960 Doncaster's BR works would build 10 DC electric locos, 3 AC electric locos, 28 204hp diesel shunters, 75 electric multiple unit vehicles and 16 freight wagons.

*By late 1996 Grace Hempsall had lived in Doncaster for 84 of her 86 years.*

*"I was brought up in Hexthorpe near the main entrances to the Plant Works, one at Kirk Street and the other in Crimpsall Road where we lived.*

*"Next-door to us was a cabinet maker who worked at the Plant, as did a great number of people*

*"Those coming from farther afield used to cycle and I can remember hundreds of bicycles at coming and leaving times of 8am and 5.30pm*

*"My father, who died in 1927, cleaned the gas lamps on all the stations along the main line between Doncaster and Newark. There were lots of smaller stations then, about 10 in all - all gas.*

After being withdrawn from service, several old GNR Atlantic locos found alternative work at Doncaster Plant.

Above: The frames and wheels of some were used until the 1960s as boiler carriers. Works pilot, J50 No. 68972 manoeuvres the boiler of Britannia No. 70039 *Sir Christopher Wren* on the frames of one ex-Atlantic on 18th September, 1961.. *(Peter Rose)*

Below: The only place where you could see a line-up of GN Atlantics in 1953 was from the river bank at the back of the works. On 17th May, from left, the remains of Nos. 4444, 3296, 4437, 4434 and 4413 were being used as stationary boilers. *(Neville Stead)*

**Top:** For several years, Atlantics Nos. 3274 and 3285 were used as stationary boilers for the Crimpsall shop as seen on 26th November, 1950.

In 1952 and 53 two new steam raising plants were commissioned, one alongside the Crimpsall and one alongside the main carriage paint shop which presumably rendered the Atlantic boilers redundant. *(R.H. Fullagar / N. E. Stead collection)*

**Centre:** An Atlantic chassis supporting a Gresley Pacific or V2 boiler used as a stationary boiler on 16th January, 1961. *(Peter Rose)*

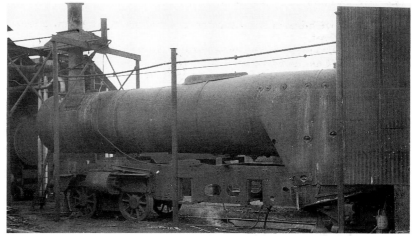

**Bottom:** Gracing the Plant with its elegance in early BR days was ex-Great Eastern F4 2-4-2T No. 7162 from Melton Constable. *(Official photo / Derek Porter collection)*

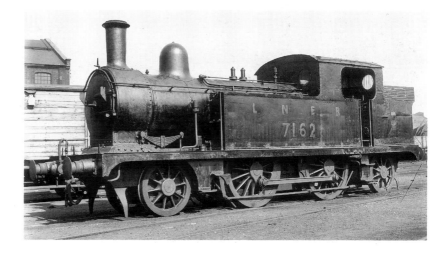

Above: 14th October, 1957 was a momentous day for the Plant. It was the day that this brand new locomotive was outshopped. BR Standard Class 4 2-6-0 was not only the last of its class but it was the last of over 2,000 steam locomotives designed and built at Doncaster Works. *(Derek Porter)*

Below: After 76114 the Plant concentrated on building main line electric locos and diesel shunters but in 1970 it completed three 1,350hp diesel locomotives for Northern Ireland Railways on behalf of the Hunslet Engine Company in Leeds.
These engines were specially for the Belfast-Dublin Enterprise express and No.101 is pictured taking shape in the new build erecting shop. *(Derek Porter)*

## SHORT MEMORIES

**3-5.2.66:** B1 61250 is on the 8.52am from Hull each day.

**23.4.66:** B1s 61042/ 1121/58/1250/1329/60/ 1406; O4s 63653/781/ 85 /818/858; WDs 90001/2/ 13/18/37/63/75/148/154 /6/369/410/37/71/538/51/ 636/75/709; and 9Fs 92182/3/2201 all withdrawn marking the end of steam at Doncaster.

**25.6.66:** A railtour to Scotland is hauled into Doncaster by SR Pacific 35026 *Lamport & Holt Line*. 35026 is serviced at Carr Loco and empties the coaling plant, becoming the last steam loco to be coaled there.

**26.6.66:** The return working of the above arrives behind preserved A3 *Flying Scotsman* and 35026 works it forward.

A4 No. 60009 *Union of South Africa* was the last steam locomotive to officially receive a heavy general repair at the Plant. It is seen here ready for its return to service on 6th November, 1963.
Some say that a WD 2-8-0 was really the last but was considered too mundane to mark such an occasion.
(*Derek Porter*)

Steam locomotives continued to receive cosmetic restoration for preservation in the national collection, after which they were placed in store or sent to Clapham Transport Museum in London.
One of those chosen for glory instead of oblivion was ex-GE J17 0-6-0 No. 65567, seen having just emerged from the paint shop resplendent in LNER livery.
No. 1217, as it had become, was put into secure store in the former engine shed at Hellifield.
(*Derek Porter*)

During 1963, A4 *Mallard* was restored to the pre-war LNER livery it was wearing when it broke the world speed record, complete with driving wheel valances and garter blue paintwork. It shines in the works yard before going to Clapham .
(*Derek Porter*)

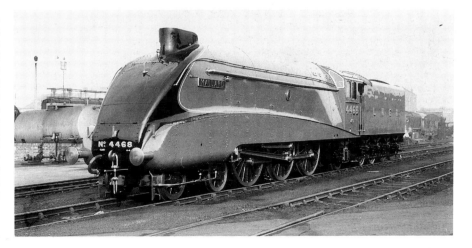

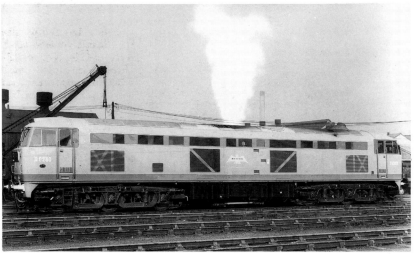

During the early 1960s, many new and prototype diesel locomotives were tested at Doncaster, new BR locomotives going there for acceptance trials.

Top: The 1961-built Yorkshire Engine Co. prototype 600hp diesel hydraulic 0-8-0 *Taurus* passes the loco weigh house while undergoing shunting trials in the works yard. *(Derek Porter)*

Centre: The 2,700hp Brush prototype D0280 *Falcon* was under test at the Plant on 12th October, 1961. *(BR Photo/Derek Porter collection)*

Bottom: Countless engines met their end in the Doncaster works scrap yard, from the oldest GNR types to the Deltics. Departmental Class Y3 Sentinel loco No. 7 (ex-68166) shunted at Boston sleeper works until making its final journey to the Plant in 1963. *(Derek Porter)*

**How the mighty are fallen.**
**Class B17/4 4-6-0 No. 61656** *Leeds United* **was built at Doncaster in 1936 and reduced to scrap there early in 1960.** *(Derek Porter)*

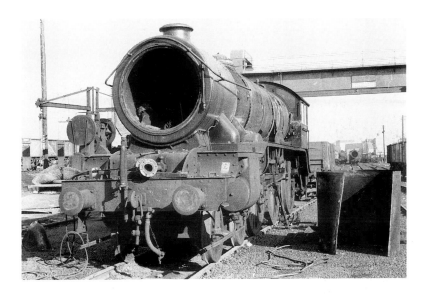

*In 1966 engines overhauled at the Plant were run-in on the 3.50am Belmont Sidings-York Yard freight, returning with the 6.48am from Dringhouses, the 18.00 Keith-Doncaster goods, or light engine.*

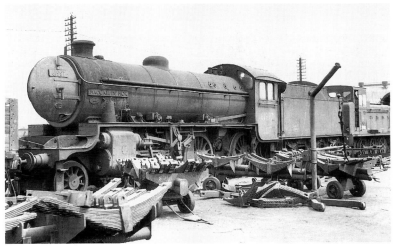

**Reined in from the Highlands of Scotland. K1/1 2-6-0 No.** *61997 MacCailin Mor* **still with nameplates and works plates intact but about to meet its doom in 1962.**
**No. 61997 was a 1945 2-cylinder rebuild of one of Gresley's K4s and formed a prototype for the 70 K1s which followed from 1949 onwards.**
**With it is Barclay 204hp 0-6-0 diesel shunter D2402 from Boston.**
*(Derek Porter)*

*The 2,000th locomotive built at Doncaster was A2/3 Pacific No. 60500 Edward Thompson, outshopped in 1946.*

**Made redundant by electrification on their London, Tilbury and Southend line, these ex-LMS Stanier 3-cylinder 2-6-4Ts were awaiting their end in 1962.**
**Central to the picture and looking rather too smart for the scrapman is 42511.** *(Derek Porter)*

Down Decoy yard was closed and lifted during 1995 and by the end of 1996 a new terminal for mail trains was taking shape there.

The yard was latterly used for wagon load coal traffic.

In January, 1990 English Electric Type 3 No. 37212 was making up an afternoon wagonload coal service to Mossend.

*(S. J. Chapman)*

# MODERN MEMORIES

Below: From the 1970s Belmont yard was dedicated to the wagonload Speedlink air-braked freight service and marshalling there ceased upon closure of the Speedlink network in the early 1990s. The yard continued to be used for storing wagons and redundant locomotives. In 1996 the English Welsh and Scottish Railway installed new facilities there for loading and discharging wagon load coal and other minerals.

In January, 1990, 350hp shunter No. 08418 was marshalling a long rake of ferry vans ready for departure on an afternoon Speedlink service.

*Even after steam has gone and modernisation and rationalisation have had their way, there will always be something interesting happening on the railway in a place like Doncaster.*

BELMONT SIDING... on the Down side of the line near Balby Junction box and affords access to British Ropes, Arnold's and Darlington Fencing Co.'s sidings, must not be used when it is dark or during fog and falling snow except in emergency on instructions from the inspector at Belmont Siding who must arrange for a shunter to accompany the guard. *ER Sectional Appendix* 1968

**Top:** The changes at Carr Loco since the end of steam were not too obvious in this June 1981 view of a Class 37 stood outside the running shed. *(Malcolm Roughley)*

**Centre:** Inside the shed were, on the left, Class 08 350hp shunters 08114 and 08745. *(Malcolm Roughley)*

**Bottom:** Bridge Junction was simplified during the 1970s remodelling. Shortly afterwards, a pair of English Electric Type 1s, 20029 leading, round the curve from St. James Junction with a train of empty tippler wagons. *(Derek Porter)*

During the diesel era Carr Loco was home to a fleet of unique Blackstone engined Class 10 diesel shunters. All were withdrawn by the early 1970s.

Above: The view from Hexthorpe Road bridge in 1975, nearly 15 years before electrification. Brush Type 4 No. 47461 departs with an Up Inter-City while an ex-works Woodhead line Class 76 electric stands outside the Plant. *(Adrian Booth)*

Below: Memories of freezing days following the last Deltics in 1981. Enthusiasts brave the cold as 55009 *Alycidon* enters platform 8 with a northbound railtour on 29th December *(Derek Porter)*

## SHORT MEMORIES

**1.8.66:** Coal trains to south of London are switched from the GN to the Midland line.

**1.5.68:** *Flying Scotsman* trying to re-enact its first King' Cross-Edinburgh non-stop run in 1928 is almost halted by a broken rail near Doncaster.

**22.11.70:** 60,000 people pack into the Plant when preserved A2 60532 is renamed *Blue Peter* by Valery Singleton and Peter Purvis of the children's TV programme.

**3.7.88:** *Mallard* is back in steam and celebrates 50 years since its 126mph record by hauling a special from Doncaster to Scarborough.

**Right:** On 31st July, 1983 English Electric Type 1s 20179 and 20191 brought the Plymouth to Scarborough White Rose Rambler railtour under the works footbridge and into platform 8.

One of the Swindon-built Class 123 DMUs used on Hull-Doncaster-Sheffield-Manchester services at the time is just right of the leading engine.
*(Stephen Chapman)*

Locomotives will enter Carr Diesel depot at Carr box, thence travel over the Down engine line to the north end, entering the depot via the one way spring hand points in the north spur. ..Outgoing locomotives will depart via the spur in the Up engine line at Carr box.
*ER Sectional Appendix 1968.*

**Left: Making its main line comback following restoration to green livery, English Electric Type 4 No. D200 (40122) leaves Doncaster with the King's Cross-Carlisle Hadrian Pullman special on Sunday 31st July, 1983.**
*(S. J. Chapman)*

**Right:** In 1987 Brush Type 4 No. 47522 was repainted LNER apple green and named *Doncaster Enterprise* to mark the opening of the Crimpsall as a 'Level Five' maintenance depot. On 1st October, two days before the open day at which it was officially named, 47522 awaits the application of its number and BR Parcels business logo following a component exchange overhaul and repaint in the Crimpsall.
*(Stephen Chapman)*

Above: During 1980 the National Railway Museum's NER 2-2-4T *Aerolite* received a repaint at the Plant where it is seen in the locomotive paint shop. The paint shop cat seems more interested in the wheelbarrow, though. *(Derek Porter)*

Below: Unless there are some dramatic changes in the Plant's fortunes, the BR 3,300hp Class 58s will have been the last main line locomotives built at Doncaster. The final one, No. 58050, was out-shopped in April, 1987 and named *Doncaster Locomotive Works*. Here, an unidentified 58 takes shape in the new build erecting shop. *(Derek Porter)*